The Galileo Moment

How global market leaders
differentiate from the rest
of the pack

Elizabeth Jayanti, Ph.D.

Dedication

This book is dedicated to Archimedes, Galileo, Joseph Losey and to all of the heroes who have lived their *Galileo Moment*, and to all of those who have yet to live it.

Contents

Acknowledgements

"All this is possible only through the blood, sweat, and tears of a number of people… beneath the surface are thousands and thousands of others." – Michael Collins, *Apollo 11 Astronaut.*

A special thank you to all the participants of my research study who shared the gifts of their time and wisdom, providing me with their perspectives, insights, and experiences. Their generosity of spirit was overwhelming and I cannot thank them enough. It was only with their help that my journey was made possible.

1 | The Galileo Moment

"I believe in Brechtian theater, which is basically reality, seen toughly and lyrically but communicating a particular point of view." –Joseph Losey

I don't know about you, but Galileo has always fascinated me. I admired Galileo's courage in standing up to the Inquisition, defending what he knew to be true *based on data and his own observations*. Galileo built a highly effective telescope that improved upon the technology of his day. At the time, Galileo had peered through his telescope and observed the stars—he saw that the earth was not the center of the solar system. It was a dangerous observation.

Before Galileo, it was common wisdom that the earth was the center of the universe. Plato had written works hypothesizing a geocentric model of the universe. Aristotle had said that "Man (kind) was the measure of all things," and placed the earth at the universe's center.

Ptolemy argued strongly that the earth was the center of the universe. The pope endorsed the view, scholars took it for granted, and everyday people unquestioningly accepted the work of experts.

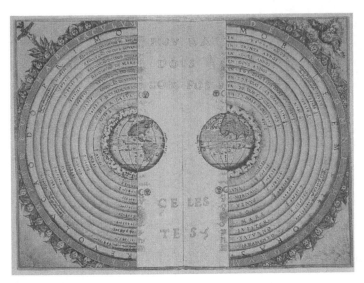

Even when Nicolaus Copernicus had hypothesized a heliocentric universe—placing the sun at the center of the universe—his views were written off as "mere theory," since there was no real evidence that humans were not the center of the universe. But Galileo's celestial vision of real data contradicted the articles of faith of the day.

Looking through his telescope, Galileo observed the data points that were the stars. What he saw must have made him nervous, knowing that even Copernicus' whispers of such a theory had resulted in strong consequences. Galileo backed away from his findings for some time, putting down the telescope, and turning his attention to the microscope to observe the very tiny and very close, in hopes of stilling his mind. Yet, there was a moment when Galileo picked up his telescope, once more peered to the sky, and decided to stand up for what he saw, no matter the cost. Despite his initial hesitance in making his observations public, Galileo gathered his courage and eventually shared this data with others. There was a moment, which I call the *Galileo Moment.*

Some have called the notion of resisting observable fact in the face of all evidence *the Galileo Effect*. But I find it problematic that resisting real world evidence is Galileo's legacy; especially since this is the antithesis of what Galileo himself stood for. What would Galileo think about being associated with ignorant mobs that are blinded to empirical data, simply because of their prior belief? Given Galileo's sacrifices in service of giving us *data-driven processes*, I would celebrate instead the *Galileo Moment*—the moment that Galileo decided to courageously stand up to the false beliefs of the masses and bring the truth of *data driven observations* to the people, even at the risk of great personal cost to himself.

Nevertheless, I was wholly unprepared for my own Galileo Moment when it finally came. Somehow, I was under the impression that a Galileo Moment was something that happened only to others; something that happened to great men who were courageous and confident and already well-established in their fields.

Instead, my Galileo Moment occurred as I—a quiet young woman of conventional impulses with a young family and a house in the suburbs—prepared to write my doctoral dissertation. As a student of organizational leadership, I had spent thousands of hours in the dusty library, seeking to find out how organizations work and innovate.

I read about model after model in pdf files, working late into the night by the steady glow of my laptop. I examined over 50 years of research first-hand and kept notes in a document that eventually stretched to 912 pages. The harder I looked, the less the supporting data seemed to describe the universe of business that the models were purportedly describing.

Like Galileo—who looking through his telescope, had observed first hand a much different solar system than the one that the academics had described—I began to observe that the universe of business was far different than the one I had been taught. My observations didn't mesh with the business school curriculum or the *Harvard Business Review* publications so popularly quoted.

First, these models focused on the *external market factors*—which no organization can control—rather than the *internal factors* which companies can change and control. If companies *could* control their market, every company would be a winner—and each company would have billions in revenue. Stock markets wouldn't dip, customers would flock, and profit would follow profit. Yet, somehow it had become a truism that companies should look to the *external market*.

Second, although these organizational instruments claimed to deal with the *organization* as a whole, they almost invariably looked only at *individuals* – be it employees, managers or leaders. But an organization is not an individual, and an individual is not an organization. Have you ever had the experience of working on a team, where the dynamic was such that you somehow achieved *more* than all of the individuals could have accomplished working alone?

Or have you ever worked on a project where the group is so dysfunctional that the final product is far worse than you would have anticipated with the group of individually intelligent people working on it? I have seen projects on either end of the spectrum—but either way, it demonstrates the fact that an organization cannot simply be measured as the sum of its individual employees.

Simply put, *organizations* are *synergistic,* a fact that is especially true in our current knowledge-based economy where work is rarely completed individually. Because teams and organizations are *synergistic,* you can't just tally up the sum of individuals and assume that the output will be equal to the sum of the group's man-hours. Some hours are more productive than others, and some groups are just smarter than others.

Third, these organizational models were assumed to be *context-independent*. Simply put, they assumed that if you applied the same model, no matter where you applied it, you would get the same, predictable results. For example, a flagging cereal manufacturer experiencing an economic downturn applying a particular model may be told to expect the exact same results that a software firm previously saw delivered. This, of course, is untrue since companies have very different contexts, cultures, and histories which shape their future directions. Because differences in initial starting points radically shape trajectories, no two companies applying a particular model are likely to deliver the exact same results. This implies that it may be important to understand the initial conditions and company culture which serve to shape your outcomes.

Finally, no one had asked anyone in industry if the models bore any resemblance to the daily reality in which they live. Reality rarely looks as neat as an imagined picture or a magic formula. Nobody had asked the question, "How do things really work?"

As I compared well over 100 models side-by-side, dimension to dimension and sample size to sample size in an spreadsheet, I came to realize that our current models were based on theories (untested hypotheses, really) that were assumed to be true—then "validated" with surveys that allowed respondents to choose option A, B, C, or D, but not options "none," or "does not apply." In other words, respondents were given the options, "yes," or "yes." And yet, we assumed these models to be fundamentally correct—holding such stock in their accuracy that we built new models on top of these shaky foundations—taking a question from one "validated" scale and building it into a new measure.

Scale was built off scale, instrument built off instrument, and *none of them* had been empirically tested. I discovered that what we have in management is a geocentric universe of management theories and models—work based on *untested assumptions* that, over the years, have solidified into *articles of faith*. Key models were assumed to be fundamentally correct, and have come to undergird *large scale* research such as the:

- OECD Innovation Survey
- European Community Innovation Survey
- U.S. Census Bureau's Survey of Manufacturers
- U.S. Census Bureau's Economic Census
- Industry Classification Codes

Millions of dollars and thousands of hours were being spent annually to prove and re-prove what were essentially *articles of faith*. Their usefulness to business practice is questionable—perhaps even detrimental, and yet, they remain unquestioned.

The old models assume:

- Market stability
- Extended product lifecycles
- No indirect competition, and high startup costs
- Staffing predictability
- Employees' work outputs producing small variability in quality and productivity
- Employee loyalty and lifetime employment
- Siloed organizations

Yet, we are currently living in what Peter Drucker called a knowledge economy. It is now estimated that 2/3 of company value is created by intangible assets (Chang & Hughes, 2012). Manufacturing has declined as a primary source of economic value, increasing the premium placed on knowledge capital. Brains have replaced brawn and briskness of production as a true source of economic value. Anyone can manufacture a product quickly—but fewer can innovate, and a large premium is placed on innovation.

The knowledge economy is marked by:

- Hyper-turbulent economic markets
- Shortened product lifecycles
- Strong indirect competition
- Lower startup costs leading to stronger direct competition
- Employees who produce highly variable results and productivity
- Employee disengagement, contract work, and layoffs
- Collaborative, inter-dependent organizations

The tools which we use in business have not caught up to our organizational reality—we are essentially relying on geocentric models to guide us in a heliocentric universe.

And, much as the geocentric models became increasingly complex and messy as it became evident that they simply didn't work, many of our business models are becoming ever-messier and more complicated. For example, the Project Management Institute's body of knowledge (PMBOK), which serves as foundation for project management (PMP) certification, was updated to include 47 processes, from 42 in the last version, and increased the number of "Input, Output, Tools and Techniques," by 19% to number 614 in all. Just like in Galileo's time when the conventional wisdom was to add extra orbits to the geocentric model to prop it up, it seems we are adding special cases and big datasets to prop up our industrial-era models.

Despite seeing the overwhelming evidence, challenging the status quo made me nervous. How could I tell a committee of professors that everything we knew as a field was wrong? Who was I to say it was wrong? What kind of risk was I taking? Selfishly, how might this effect my hope of graduating—or in the bigger picture, did that even matter?

This was my Galileo Moment. It was at once terrifying and exhilarating. Nobody wants to turn the world they know upside down—who wants to fight the universe?—but once you see the data, and the world as it is, it is hard to go back to not knowing. In our lives, each of us has a few glimpses of greatness.

There are moments—Galileo Moments—where we see with our own eyes that the world doesn't work quite the way that we were told, when the tools and theories don't work exactly the way they're supposed to, and when the mathematical equations don't add up. In these moments, we may experience an internal battle between our individual intelligence and societal pressures leaning towards tradition and obedience.

When Stanley Milgram conducted an experiment on obedience to authority, 37 out of the 40 participants followed the instructions of a gentleman wearing a lab coat over their own best judgment—even though that meant administering electric shocks to a peer who had complained of a heart condition, simply because that gentleman said that the experiment must continue. In our everyday lives, I doubt that many of us are more courageous. As Peter Thiel put it, "Courage is in even shorter supply than genius."

Many companies have gone bankrupt because of people's tendency to follow the crowd, against the face of all evidence. For example, despite customer requests and market data that computers might be the wave of the future, Smith-Corona unquestioningly followed its strategy of focusing on producing high quality typewriters—a strategy which had brought them much past success. They followed that successful strategy right into bankruptcy. How sad that nobody had the courage to stand up. By standing up in a Galileo Moment, one person can save a company or change the course of history.

At a point in the doctoral research process where almost everybody proceeds with the projects that they had planned, I went back to the basics and redesigned the study. Instead of starting with a theory-based model as so many others had done, I began asking people how things really worked. I completely overhauled my research methodology to match the emerging state of the research, and presented my plan again—this time, with great success.

I interviewed over 60 Chief Technical Officers, Chief Financial Officers, Vice Presidents, Directors, Senior Managers, technical leads, and front line employees from companies ranging from medical, consumer equipment, and robotics, to software industry giants including Google and Microsoft. The picture of organizations that emerged from our conversations was far different from the one portrayed in books, journals, and the prevalent models based on assumptions rooted in a past industrial age.

Eventually, my study received a Highly Commended Dissertation Award from the European Foundation for Management Development in an international competition, beating submissions from elite business schools around the US, Europe, and Asia! I was greatly honored to be presented with such an award.

I was pleasantly surprised again when, a bit later, my work was a finalist in the University Council of Work and Human Resource Education's Outstanding Dissertation Award. The faculty of each university in the council is allowed to select just one dissertation to represent the university, and from those select few, the finalists emerge. Reading the news along with everyone else was my first notice of this honor.

It was a delightful surprise to see that Galileo Moments can turn out well for an individual *as well as* change the world. This pleasant ending, of course, was not why I had embarked on the journey. But it was certainly a good way for the journey to end. It is my hope that readers, when presented with the opportunity, stand up and take their Galileo Moment. It is a moment that can profoundly change the world.

How To Use This Book

This book is designed to serve as a telescope—to focus your attention to the stars. By looking at star businesses, I am hoping you will look at the business data with an open mind. Each chapter focuses on a basic principle and concludes with a worksheet so that you can immediately apply the new world business principle to your own company's unique situation. By the end of the book, you will:

- Have a greater understanding of your company's culture, and limits for change
- Optimize your activities and processes to focus on what really matters
- Generate better business results by doing less
- Have a new understanding of risk
- Focus on activities rather than industry, preventing not only direct, but also indirect, competitors from taking market share

Exercise I: Preparing for Your Galileo Moment

STEP 1		**CHECK YOUR LENSES** Am I looking at real-world data & evidence, or am I filtering the data?
STEP 2		**LOOK INSIDE** What additional data do I need in order to make an informed decision?
STEP 3		**LOOK OUTSIDE** Who else does this impact?
STEP 4		**LOOK BEYOND** What is the risk of continuing to do what I have been doing?

What lenses am I looking through? Am I looking at real-world data, or am I filtering information?

What additional data do I need to make an informed decision?

Who else does this impact?

What is the risk of continuing to do what I have been doing?

If I intend to make a change, how do I know it is the right change? Am I following a scientific method in a data-driven manner when making changes, or am I making multiple changes such that I cannot measure the impact of those changes and make adjustments?

2 | A New Map of the Business Universe

"Measure what is measurable, and make measurable what is not so." –Galileo Galilei

Like Galileo, I have observed the stars, and hope to share this data with you. The assumed map of the business universe—how companies work, innovate, grow, transform, change, adapt to markets, and learn from customers—is nothing like it has been depicted in the previous studies. From the way that big firms innovate, to the way that companies make decisions, a lot of what you learned in your MBA is no longer true. While management scholars and gurus were busy quantifying theoretical models of the way companies work, based on industrial-era assumptions, nobody bothered to take a look at real companies—nobody looked at the stars for data points. Nobody asked the question, "How do things really work?" Instead, many were too busy proving themselves right with large quantitative studies and giant sample sizes validating their hypotheses, but failed to examine the underlying assumptions. Despite being "validated" with large sample sizes, these instruments are not fundamentally valid. A majority of research coming from elite universities and consulting firms are now the benchmark for global business change, and yet, these tools fail to give voice to real practice.

In many cases, instruments are built around management theories. These theories serve as a framework, and question sets are built around structures such as an acronym, a quadrant, or a taxonomy. Questions are developed to fit and describe the dimensions of the framework. Researchers generate lists of questions, primarily through pulling questions about similar topics from other researchers' instruments. In many cases, researchers assume that someone else has asked real people about their work, and collected the data in a structured and replicable way—and in many cases, this assumption is unfounded.

These lengthy lists of questions are then frequently reduced through Delphi testing, where committees of colleagues decide how well these particular questions fit the framework of an assumed theoretical model. Subsequently, a finalized question set is sent out to respondents. Respondents may select closed answers, such as selecting option "A, B, C, or D," but may not say, "I have no idea what you're talking about." In other words, respondents may confirm or reject specific question items, but not the overall framework or structure, which stands as theorized.

And as more and more respondents send in their responses, and the results accumulate, these instruments take on a halo of validity around them—20,000 people can't be wrong. Yet, as any beginning student in Research Methods learns in the first few classes, big sample sizes don't matter if you're not asking the right questions. 20,000 people were not asked about how they worked—20,000 people filled in bubble answers on a sheet of paper to questions which may or may not have any basis in reality.

I am not asking you to believe blindly in yet another fad model; I only ask that you observe the data with me, and bring an open mind. I invite you to draw your own conclusions. If your observations line up with mine, I believe that these observations will shift the way you think and lead forever. I hope that they will encourage you to take your Galileo moment.

I interviewed 61 professionals in 13 of the world's leading organizations. These were companies that were listed on Fortune Magazine's and Fast Company's most innovative company lists, and included such leaders as:

- Google
- Microsoft
- 3M
- Marvin Windows
- Ecolab
- Dassault Systemes
- and several others

Participants included Chief Technical Officers, Chief Financial Officers, Vice Presidents, Directors, Managers, and Front-line employees at locations across the globe.

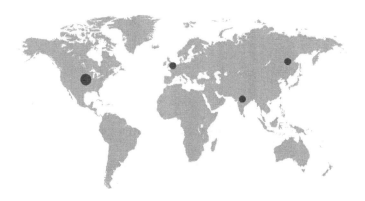

Although people may not have heard of or think of companies like Marvin Windows or Ecolab when they first think of innovation, these companies are leaders in their fields, have survived much longer than the 5 years within which most companies fail, and have strong earnings. I now believe that it is important not only to examine successful technology companies when studying innovation, but to view innovation across industries ranging from finance to manufacturing, robotics to automotive, and from medical to chemical. Indeed, it is only by viewing innovation across the entire spectrum of possibility that we are better able to understand innovation in its essence.

In our half-hour interviews, the participants were extremely open with me, and willing to share their experiences. For example:

In the words of a Vice President:

> *"I just had to make a very tough decision a few minutes ago; one of our executives violated the trust of the company by forging a document. At the end of the day, it didn't cost us anything, but I mean... there is no black and white variance when it comes to integrity."*

In the words of a front line technical employee in a regulated industry:

> *"Typically, there's no product, in the age that we live in, that is all of a sudden just popping up... that a company has been trying to develop for 10 years and then releases it on the market. It just doesn't work like that because everything is documented, as soon as anybody files for any [patent] applications, people know what's going down out there, so that's what you see. You don't typically see one rabbit in front of the pack. It's kind of [that] the whole industry swings together."*

In the words of a Director:

> *"My experience has been that manufacturing environments often times give rise to people that are more collaborative and the reason being is that when you're in a 24/7 operation, it's very difficult to not be relying on others to help you get your job done."*

Demographics

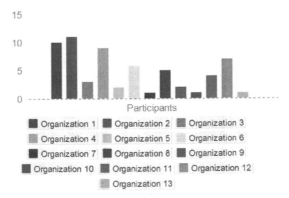

Participants

- Organization 1
- Organization 2
- Organization 3
- Organization 4
- Organization 5
- Organization 6
- Organization 7
- Organization 8
- Organization 9
- Organization 10
- Organization 11
- Organization 12
- Organization 13

Gender

Role

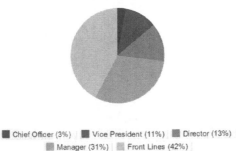

- Chief Officer (3%)
- Vice President (11%)
- Director (13%)
- Manager (31%)
- Front Lines (42%)

Their insights were at once startling and puzzling. At first, I did not know what to make of them. When you ask a question about whether a firm is in the *high-tech space* or the *cost-effective space*, based on everything that is known in today's management literature, and are met with the response, "Let me explain to you, that's not the way things work at all," from the Vice President, it's a little hard to know what to make of it. But when several Vice Presidents, Directors, and Managers across companies and locations around the world tell you the same thing—you know you're probably on to something.

The New Map of the Business Universe

Now that we have GPS satellites, google maps, and digital images of places which can be sent to our mobile phones at the touch of a button, it seems almost impossible to get lost (nevertheless, some still do!). It is hard to imagine life without maps that are based on real world data and real-time information. Maps tell us about the ground that others have trod before us, where to turn, and what route to follow.

It is hard to imagine the courage it must have taken for early explorers to follow maps that depicted dragons swimming along the edges of the earth to swallow you up if you made a mistake. Or maps of the moon that assumed that its surface was as smooth as a pearl or made out of green cheese. But when you think about it, those maps are a lot like the maps of business we have today. The maps of the business universe are fantastical in their imagination, having been most frequently "theoretically derived"—that is, based on little more than the gauzy fabric of ephemeral thoughts; the same fabric that was used to spin the maps of the unknown world depicting dragons and sea monsters.

Business professionals today require no less courage than that of the map-less explorers who went before as they embark on journeys filled with determination, optimism, hope, and little idea of where they are heading. The journeys are dangerous, occur at an ever-accelerating pace, and the results are sadly predictable. It is estimated that roughly 15% of companies won't survive the first year, 30% won't survive beyond three years, and only 50% of companies will survive the first five years (Bjerke & Hultman, 2002). These fearless captains of industry may as well be journeying into the stars for all the risk and unknowns involved.

While markets are constantly shifting, with companies competing based on specific strengths in niche areas, much of a company's journey has to do with adapting itself to its market environment. Looking across a wide range of companies—each successful in its own right—what I found was that there is a core process for high performance. The inner workings of a company and its external performance are interconnected. By understanding these interconnected pieces, and how companies internalize raw data from their environment and transform it into innovation, we have a map for business success.

The Map to Success

It is much easier to follow a map than to blaze a trail through an unknown jungle yourself. It involves less risk, entails less fear, and means that you can focus on the more important parts of your journey. To hold a map in your hands makes possible what previous explorers left unimagined.

I set on a journey to explore learning organizations—that is, those organizations that consistently generate remarkable value and are characterized by:

- Synergy based on collective actions and common interpretation among team members (Hutchins, 1991;

Love, Huang, Edwards, & Irani, 2004; Weick & Roberts, 1993)

- Free exchange of information (Snell, 2001)
- Continual improvement (Argyris, 1999; Snell, 2001)
- Increased value and innovation

From this journey, a picture emerges that is not simply a compilation of thoughts and ideas from individual industry leaders, but a distillation of the essence of innovation which none of the leaders held individually. Through my familiarity with both the research and the practice, I was able to boil down the data into a recipe for success.

What I found was that leading *learning organizations*—regardless of industry—essentially followed the same process of *becoming*—whether that meant changing, adapting, growing, acquiring, or innovating. While the mapped process appears deceptively simple, it is radically different from the paths that organizations have been told to follow by pricey consultants or ivory tower researchers.

Although most organizational instruments look at individuals within an organization—their personal preferences, their individual strengths, or independent learning styles—I quickly found that the most successful organizations ignored the noise and were holistic in their thinking, viewing their organizations solely at the organizational level. This made sense, because belonging to an organization motivates people as a group apart from their own individual—and sometimes selfish—interests. Employees don't do things like stay late after work, work on weekends to finish projects, or stay on-call until the wee hours of the morning because it is in their own *personal interest* or because it matches their *individual personality, strength,* or *work style.* They do it because *others depend on them* to get the job done, and they are motivated by doing something *greater than themselves.*

Just as employees sometimes sacrifice their free time for the greater good, people also *adapt* to their organization's ways of doing things—the documentation specialist, the parts representative, and the manufacturing engineer all work together to put things into a coherent process. Now, this process may not match the documentation specialists' natural way of ordering things—but she does it because it makes sense in the larger scheme of things. She learns and adapts her flow to match the way things were done in the past, and to the structures that are in place because the document repository is arranged in a certain way. She understands that new documents must be navigable and consistent in format with the old ones, to make others' jobs more efficient. Individuals in an organization learn the *company's ways of doing things* and adjust their own practice to match the behaviors that are rewarded. **In today's workplace, people's adaptability is dramatically underestimated.** You don't have to ask people what they would *prefer to* do in order to understand what they *would do* when push comes to shove. Just like smaller satellites orbit larger planets, individual employees often fall into alignment with larger organizational plans.

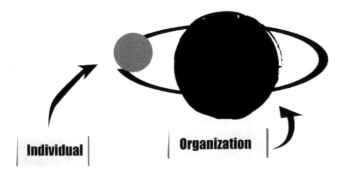

Individual | Organization

This suggests that many would-be-mapmakers have been looking at the wrong unit entirely—studying tiny satellites in great detail, when it is far more important to understand the organization that is being orbited. Just as a small satellite is more likely to be thrown out of its orbit than a large planet, **organizational ways of doing things are more stable over time than individual ways of doing things.** Organizational ways of being and doing have been shown to persistently impact companies even after the exit of organization members (Ford, 2008; Levitt & March, 1988; Sinkula, 1994) or changes in organizational systems, processes, and products (Weick, 1969).

A company's way of learning and doing is impactful over the very long-term—serving to persistently impact organizational culture and actions even after the exit of several generations of employees. The work that people do lives on long after they are gone, exhibited in the continuing patterns of the company culture. In the words of a manufacturing company trainer:

> I did a lot of lean six-sigma type projects where you'd run into a situation where you obviously see that there is some opportunity for improvement in a certain process, but no one can explain why a certain requirement is in place that increases the process cycle time by X number of hours, and the people who put that in place are no longer with the company, and the people who are there don't know why, and the people who are assembling the products don't know why, and it can't be changed.

Novices also tend to acquire expert's ways of doing things, since they are easily able to see who has been successful by looking at who is rewarded—and they emulate those behaviors and practices. People tend to seek respect and achievement. Rare indeed would be the employee who actually seeks to be a low performer. Low performance is often a reaction that is the result of frustration with company conditions. People want to look good in the eyes of others, and achieve whatever will gain them respect. In the words of safety manager:

> If your management or your leaders think that it's not important to train on safety because it's not a big deal, safety's not really our priority, we're worrying about making parts, and things like that, that trickles down the line faster than you can think because if they give the perception that it's not important, every guy on the floor immediately knows that, and you can see it; facial expressions and things like that will give it away every single time. Whatever the supervisor or the manager does not think is important, the guy will not do. And it's just wrecked my day, you know. It's very tough to overcome that.

Organizational learning is much more *collective* than people have typically believed. But this also means that it is more stable and *predictable* than people have previously considered. This means that, as a process, it is more *manageable*, given the right tools. The payoffs to managing change and learning are immense.

If we are to meaningfully understand organizations, we must step back and view them as whole systems. Like visitors to an art museum who step up too close to an impressionist's canvas, what is seen up close in organizations often does not make sense. Looking at an organization as a group of individuals is like looking at a confusing jumble of dots of paint on an impressionistic canvas. It is only by stepping back and seeing the whole, that we can understand the bigger picture clearly.

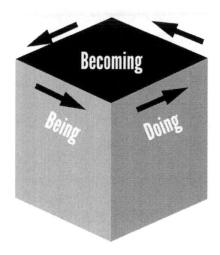

It all begins with company culture. Company culture constitutes a way of **being**. A company's culture is so much a part of the day-to-day life that it isn't always apparent to people within the company. Asking about company culture is a lot like asking a fish inside a goldfish bowl to describe his surroundings—it isn't like anything, it just is. Company culture often defies verbal description, but may be intensely felt.

In the words of a Fortune 500 firm's Chief Technical Officer:

> I think [our company] has a very interesting culture and this was the first real job that I had; I mean, I had gone through graduate school and I had my paper boy and bag boy and dishwasher jobs before, but this was my first real adult job. It's sort of interesting to me because I don't always think of it as exceptional because I literally kind of grew up in it, but then it was spun off; after I started, I was spun off to Company B, and back then Company B was a company that had no culture. Then I came back here 4 years later and so it really heightened my sense of what I was missing,

because at Company B we were in the process of trying to figure out what the company would be about? That was a very interesting experience for me.

This *way of being* is fundamental to a company. It shapes the way that employees do things; it shapes the growth strategy, the approach to knowledge management, and means to engage employees with their work. Understanding company culture is the key to success. Company culture and organizational subculture (to use a more rigorous term, *organizational epistemology*) is far more important than national culture or generational differences, because people who work in a company are generally expected to behave in certain ways, are subject to the same processes, the same limits, the same customer expectations, and the same pressures, and hence, respond in similar ways while they are at work. Understanding company culture leads to unlocking why things are done the way that they are done in an organization, and what makes sense to the organization as a whole.

Companies have a particular perspective—mental models of the way things work, and should work, and what's worked in the past. They have experiences which they have weathered—market downturns and shifts in demand. They have successes behind them, and successes still to come. And because of these experiences, they have a particular way of making sense of the world. They apply these past experiences to new situations and settings, and they bring this culture to every new problem that they encounter.

This way of making sense—the way of *being*—influences a company's practices and what it *does*. In order to understand what a company does and why it does it—or behaves as it does—you must start by first understanding its culture. A company brings its culture to every practice, every product, every service, and every market.

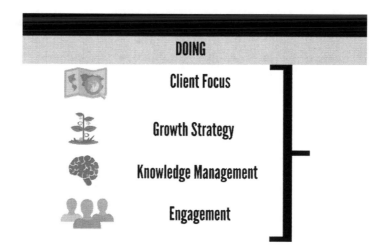

DOING

Client Focus

Growth Strategy

Knowledge Management

Engagement

Every company—no matter how big, and no matter how small—acts to address four main concerns. Ranked in order of importance, these are: *client focus, growth strategy, knowledge management,* and *engagement.* The approach which a company takes to address these four areas constitutes a firm's way of *doing.* In this manner, each company's approach is unique.

Client focus

While many companies will initially tell you that they are there to serve the customer, the reality is much more complex. A company's activities may ultimately serve the customer, shareholder, employee, or society more broadly. Who all of this is done for—all of the product development work, all of the manufacturing labor, all of the marketing, and all of the service—significantly impacts what the results will be, and ultimately, what the organization looks like.

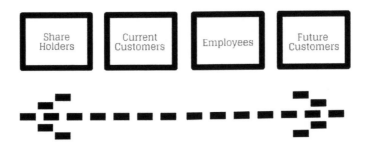

Short Term   Long Term

From my research, I found evidence of four distinct types of clients a company has—shareholders, current customers, employees, and future customers. The client focus that a company takes is not only unique in terms of *who* is being served, when push comes to shove and not everybody can get what they want, but this customer focus also shapes a company's time purview. For example, if a company is most focused on its shareholders and the bottom line, it will tend to be thinking from quarter to quarter, and perhaps to the end of the year; such companies tend to strongly focus on profitability and economic measures. But if a company is focused on its future customers, that is a much broader and longer-term view. Quarterly profits for a company focusing on future customers are not a be-all or end-all.

Shareholder Focus

Some firms intensely focused on shareholders rather than direct customers. For these firms, whether a product would generate profit was most important. To a medical device manufacturing firm's trainer:

Most of the decisions are made based on market pressure, and improvements that you see are market-driven in many ways because you know, you don't make improvements unless they contribute to the bottom line, right?

His colleague, an engineering manager concurred:

We're never going to do a project that you look at it and you say, 'oh gee, we're never going to recoup the money,' or 'there's no market but let's just pump a lot of money into it'. I mean that doesn't happen like that.

Companies often shift their focus from internal R&D to external acquisitions under pressure from shareholders since innovation is misperceived as "risky," while direct purchases are assumed to be a "sure thing." Some companies abandon R&D in their core markets entirely.

For these firms, continuing shareholder investments drive the support of continued research and development and operations, supporting the firm's mission. By focusing on keeping shareholders satisfied, such companies are making a bet that this strategy will enable them to better serve their customers, through gaining more investment of funds and increasing cash flow. In such a company, employee satisfaction is not a major focus, since development activities cost money, don't interest shareholders, and are not viewed as profitable. Employees are expected to deliver on a shareholder focused strategy, whether that involves working late or putting in extra effort. But despite this expectation, many (not all) such companies are readily willing to cut their workforce, restructure operations, move operations overseas, or automate production if it means hitting shareholder targets. In the extreme, shareholder-focused companies will sometimes even shift strategy and market focus in order to meet shareholder forecasts.

For example, before IPO, a Minnesota company built tremendous market value by focusing on fast delivery of low-volume injection-molded plastic parts. When it went to IPO in 2012, the 3D printing market was getting all the attention. In fact, the company's shares rose because of investor confusion and a misunderstanding that the firm was also in the 3D printing space. After the IPO, the company came under pressure from investors to show new products in the 3D printing space against the wishes of its original co-founders, who did not feel that 3D printing met the needs of their niche customers. Nevertheless, as soon as a new CEO came on board, the company began acquiring 3D printing firms rather than continuing to focus on internal R&D. Only time will tell if this strategy is successful.

Current Customer Focus

Some extremely successful organizations took a customer-centered approach focused on serving current customers. In the words of a manufacturing firm's director: "I would say customers come first, because without the customers, we're not going to have any employees, so there's a big focus on customers." By serving current customers and providing what they want and need today, these firms were able to produce products and services that primarily delivered value for customers. By focusing on customers, such firms were able to achieve customer loyalty (and repeat business) as well as profitability.

Pursuit of a customer-centric strategy involved high levels of service and support, a close eye on the supply chain to hit consumer pricing targets, and occasionally, some resonance and identification with the customer—a sense of really putting themselves in the customer's shoes. In the words of a sports vehicle manufacturer's Engineering Manager:

> People that work here do so because they love to ride on off-road vehicles. They're passionate about the product, and are ultimately the end consumers as well.

While companies pursuing a customer-centric strategy had a lot of upsides, on the flipside, they tended to be limited in the extent to which they could stretch innovation to the cutting edge. Many of these firms were so focused on their customers that they didn't want to alienate the current customer bases—some of which were rather large markets. As one manufacturing company's Director put it:

> Innovation is certainly a leading ingredient for growth here; but a lot of times, we're applying those technologies for what the customer wants and needs. So it might be a tried-and-true technology that hasn't been put on an off-road vehicle. We tend to not develop brand new technologies and put them on brand new products; [there's] crazy risk with that, but maybe take something that's out there already in terms of the technology and applying it. That's been a great recipe for us.

Employee Focus

A couple of companies I spoke with focused on their employees, whom they viewed as internal customers. Admittedly, this is a unique strategy—in fact, it isn't found in the academic management literature at all. An HR Vice President described his building products firm's philosophy this way:

> It sort of fits this company's view that we're not here for tomorrow, we're here for generations. We're here

for our communities and customers. At the end of the day, whether the company makes money is not the be all and end all.

At another consumer products manufacturer, there was a significant focus on employees, even though the firm was a large publicly held company. To its Chief Financial Officer:

> I think it starts with the employee, I really do. I believe that we feel as an organization that if your employees are treated well, they will seek the best solutions for the customer.

This was evident in the culture, down the front lines. An environmental health and safety manager described his company's focus this way:

> You're still around guys and machinery and equipment and stuff like that, right? But you feel like people, its family.

By focusing on their employees, these companies perceived that they were ultimately helping to better serve customers, because happy employees may be more willing to go the extra mile and build relationships with customers. These relationships help employees to gain goodwill and access to information which they might not otherwise be privy to, and this information can serve as a form of competitive advantage. By understanding the customers better than the competition, these firms are able to produce better and more innovative products, or to provide better customer support. This knowledge is a source of market power.

Future Customer Focus

In general, I found that software firms often take the broadest view—and seek to serve and support not only the customers who have purchased a particular product, but all those who may *someday* purchase the product. For these firms, not everything makes direct bottom-line financial sense, because they rightly see that bottom-line thinking is only a short-term measure. Such firms aim at much longer-term success and invest in approaches which pay off only indirectly, and only over the very long term. By focusing on a future customer base, these firms often seek to serve society more broadly.

In the words of an HR Director at a well-known high tech firm:

> My first week here, I had a meeting with sales, and the head of sales was asking about this $30 million dollar spend or whatever it was, to photograph the forest in Finland from a satellite so that we could put it on to maps. And the question around that was that it was a huge amount of money to spend and there's no value. How many people are going to use it? Who's going to make money selling ads around the forest of Finland? But it's one of the things where our founders would say that it makes it a better product. Yeah, we're not going to make the money back on that specific forest that we photographed, but you could argue over time, that this makes us the place to go for everything and it starts to build the reputation that we're not nickling and diming around.

A learning and development professional at a different established software firm took a slightly different view, "When you have an installed customer base, you have installed products in the market, you can't really stop supporting those, otherwise you risk losing those customers in the future." This attempt at mass-appeal leads to far different results than an approach which focuses only on direct and current customers.

Because software firms realize that their early adopters are significantly different from the customer users who will be purchasing their products later (for example, your mother or grandmother), they try to build with a future customer in view. This results in products which are scalable, intuitive, visually appealing, and easy-to-use.

Depending upon which of the four client-types a company focuses on, they will:

- Take a different approach to the employment contract
- Have a longer- or shorter-term time view
- Track different metrics
- Utilize different marketing strategies

Growth Strategy

Growth strategy is secondary to shaping the organization. Which growth strategy a firm takes out into the market is significantly shaped by its internal culture. While some companies grow significantly through mergers and acquisitions (M&A), other firms shy away from the rapid growth approach because they care deeply about protecting the company culture. Company growth strategies range from significant M&A activity, to growth through human capital, to pace of organic growth, or even growth through efficient operations.

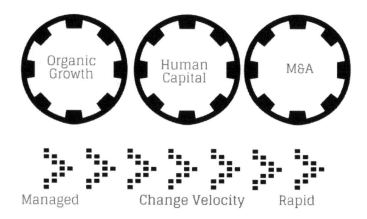

Organic Growth Human Capital M&A

Managed Change Velocity Rapid

To a consumer product manufacturer firm's Vice President:

> M&A's have a significant disruptive factor to your culture if you're not very careful about it, so we tend to focus on organic growth. And I would say to date we have been more opportunistic in our acquisitions, either extending product lines or adjacent markets that we can go after. But we always look very diligently at how that will fit into our culture.

To a software company's Program Manager:

> M&A has been very strongly outlaid maybe to the detriment of the organization because the culture is so important. Whenever you do M&A you sort of dilute the culture, right? And you evolve the culture, for lack of a better word, and if you really hold the culture in esteem then you're very worried about quick evolutionary steps to that culture.

Other firms were actively involved in growth through M&As. To a consumer products manufacturing firm's Developer:

> I would say our CEO seems to be focused most on mergers and acquisitions first, second would be operational focus, and third would be people.

To a Technical Director, who managed a software firm:

> I would say [the focus is on] M&A because every year we are making some kind of acquisition, and yeah, we do pretty well. There's a lot of cash I guess, and there's a good vision from the high up management in terms of where we should be going, so they are not only focusing on organic growth, but also mergers and acquisitions. But in general, I think the growth focus is more on the mergers.

Between these two extremes were the firms who wished to squeeze more results out of the resources that they already had—such as by continually improving operational efficiencies. Such companies did not necessarily seek this strategy simply to protect their company culture, since this strategy was used equally by firms protecting their company culture as well as those firms which sought to better serve shareholders and which did not hesitate to lay off employees to meet financial targets. In my opinion, operational effectiveness strategies are perhaps the most limited of growth strategies, because there is only so much efficiency a company can squeeze out of the same resources, without developing or expanding new ones. Gains through efficiency are not limitless; like wringing water out of a sponge, eventually the sponge will run dry. It is not a question if, but when, this will happen.

A firm's growth strategy is a lot like a compass—guiding the direction of where a firm will go. Which direction a firm is headed significantly influences the terrain that will be crossed, the speed of the journey, and the ultimate endgame for the company; whether that desired outcome is privatization, public stock purchase, or slow and steady growth as a path to market dominance.

Knowledge Management Approach

Believe it or not, innovation is not just about learning something new. It's also practical—it's about applying that knowledge, and keeping that knowledge on hand so that it serves as a tangible resource that can be drawn on in the future. A company's approach to knowledge management essentially influences whether the firm will be highly innovative, or continue to do the same things over and over again while expecting different results.

Imagine for a moment that you learned something new today, and then immediately forgot it the next. And that every new skill or tidbit you learned, you immediately proceeded to forget the next day. Your friends and family might start to worry about you. Now, if your long-term memory never absorbed any new information, it is evident that you would spend all of your time constantly re-learning. You would probably never get anything new accomplished, but would be trapped in doing the same old things over and over again. It would be a terrible fate—being both dull and painful simultaneously. As with many things, the ancient Greeks had a story which well captures the feeling. In Greek mythology, Prometheus steals fire for humans from the gods. But the gods on Mount Olympus are angered, and decide to punish him. As his punishment, he is chained to a rock, and his liver is eaten by vultures each day. At night, his liver grows back, and it is eaten again in the morning.

Many companies are trapped in a process of constantly re-learning information. Because they get trapped in this cycle, they never do much innovating—they're constantly engaged in re-learning what they already knew. As employees retire or leave, new people come aboard and try to figure out just how to do what's already been done.

Learning organizations tend to do a better job with storing knowledge—locking it away into the long-term organizational memory. Knowledge management is the process of taking something as ephemeral as clouds and capturing it for future reuse. Companies do this through four distinct approaches—through documentation, the use of stories or folklore, accessing tacit or tribal knowledge, or through internal networking and knowing who to go to for key information.

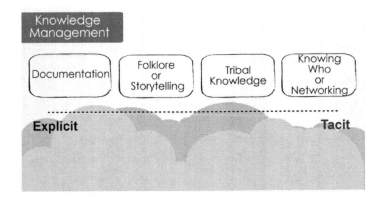

Documentation

Documentation is the most obvious and immediate way of storing knowledge and making sure that it is accessible to future members of the organization. One Product Manager described their company focus on documentation this way:

Process, quality, you know *we document what we do*, and *we do what we document*, and this is what we hold people accountable to. If it isn't written, it's not done.

When you think about it in practical terms, this is stunning—if a thing isn't documented, it isn't done! Can you imagine the level of intensity that is added to a project when you not only have to do your work, but write reports about having done the work?

He continued:

The other thing about this business, and it speaks to the process and the quality aspects, is that there is a level of bureaucracy here [that] is like none I've ever experienced before.

Documentation-oriented companies have the luxury of being able to replace employees or move employees around to different positions because "work secrets" are made rather explicit by the level of documentation; however, the pace of change and innovation tends to be relatively slow in documentation-focused companies simply because after a certain point, you can either do the work, or you can document the work, but you can't do both—heavy documentation starts cutting into the time resource for innovation.

There is certainly a balance to be struck in terms of how much documentation should be conducted. As a manufacturing firm's marketing manager framed it:

Well, it's one of those things that [if] you're trying to develop people, and they move out of their role, you still need that knowledge and in that case they may be available but they have another role that really is consuming a lot of their time, and that's probably the best case scenario, if you individually can tap into [them]. Worst case is they leave the company and things aren't captured, or at least to the degree that you [need] in order to pick up to try and figure out how to navigate forward. I'm trying to get much more formalized in terms of documentation. One of those challenges I think, [is] trying to find that happy medium where there's the past seeds to actually get the documentation done. Process mapping and documentation can be incredibly time intensive and the level of detail that one can take with things, can be inefficient to maintain in its currency. So there's been a little bit of evolution in terms of how much documentation is necessary, at what point and which processes. It's just ongoing learning for the organization.

Folklore or Storytelling

Several companies used stories of past challenges or achievements to great effect. These stories were memorable, actionable, and embedded the "what to do" in terms that people could readily remember. A large manufacturing company's Vice President described it this way:

> It's company folklore, for sure. I mean we talk about history; I find myself doing it. I talk about successes and moving our organization forward through stories of the past or things I've seen or people and how they've done things. One of the stories I use is [about] our past CEO who made some very difficult decisions with our product when we had fires that were starting from them. And I passed that along, the ethics of the decision making. How the decision was made and what was taken into account first, and you know, while you had to worry about the shareholders, we worried first

about the customer. And that helped us make the right decision, by asking certain questions along the way. But I don't have a write up that says here are the steps between 1 through 10. When I meet with my teams, I don't have the document that says you must and will do this. I tell them a story. And I tell them a story about past leaders and about how they operated. I think people connect to stories; it tends to be part of my DNA, I guess, which fits with the corporation's, so it's been good.

Tribal Knowledge

Although several firms admitted to having a base of tribal knowledge—and trying to get away from relying upon it as they transition to explicit documentation—a few companies suggested that tribal knowledge was often tacit knowledge, which was difficult to translate into words or documents. The companies which viewed tribal knowledge as primarily consisting of tacit information tended to accept that not all knowledge can be documented; and as such, these firms allowed the informal knowledge to persist as a continuing source of innovation rather than trying to eliminate it. In these cases, the tacit knowledge tended to peacefully coexist with more tangible forms. The Director of a software firm described it to me this way:

> I think there's a lot of knowledge just maintained through people, and passing information on from person to person. But we also have a lot of the processes built into tools that we're required to use, so to release a product, you have to use this tool and this tool has parameters to make sure that the right things are done at the right time.

A training professional in the same company concurred:

A lot of it is tribal knowledge; we have that social media tool and the social technology being captured, but a lot of it sits on our servers that nobody knows exist.

When asked what type of knowledge his company used, another software company's marketing manager responded this way:

Yeah, it's definitely tribal knowledge. I would say that strategy tends to be a bit more tribal like why we went into a particular business or specific opportunity. It's not always clear as to why we chose to go down a certain path, but things like the innovation pipeline and pricing business activities tend to be better documented.

A manufacturing engineer recounted a story that crystallized just how much his firm relied on tribal knowledge:

I'm trying to remember the term they use for that, there's a term, but everybody has his own little way of making that component, and they hold it pretty close, so you'll run into this problem where you can't figure out why the same part running in the same machine isn't coming out the same (in terms of quality and rate) on all three shifts? One guy always seems to have a better handle on it. You have programs on the machine; you would think that when second shift comes in and takes over, it would just continue on. But then we find out that the guy on first shift, who really has a better way of making the part, wants to keep that secret to himself. So, at three o'clock in the afternoon, he changes his machine back to run slower. We try to document it the best we can. We have our processes documented, and they're supposed to follow those processes, but we know that they don't.

Several companies described "living legends" in their midst—
those "go to" people who often served as living repositories
of company knowledge or stories. As the manger of a
financial services firm told me,

> I have only been here 18 years, well 'only', but then I
> work for one woman who's been here like 25-27 years,
> something like that, but can tell you the folklore of
> some of it. We have a guy we call the corporate
> cheerleader; he was here 40 years the day that I came in.

These key individuals served as living memories for
company knowledge that hadn't been written down. But in
order to be truly useful, relationships had to be built to
connect novices with the more experienced team members.

In order to usefully access tacit knowledge, or tap into
experience, a company has to effectively connect people in a
network. As a fortune 500 firm's marketing manager described
it:

> If I think about my own job, I think some of it is built
> into processes, and some of it's tucked in as tacit
> knowledge; it's knowledge that you have because of the
> experiences that you have behind you. It's like how
> every person will assess a problem or an opportunity
> differently, right? And so all of these filters [that you
> have] as you approach that problem will be different
> and that will be based on your own biases, they're based
> on what your history has been, they're based on what
> your education is, all kinds of different things. I think
> it's that whole that goes into this maintenance of
> knowledge or having the knowledge to address the
> problem.

This is exactly where internal networking comes in handy. A Vice President described his Fortune 500-firm's use of internal networking this way:

> The goal is to make connections because just like in your brain, your brain is only as good as your synapses for connecting different parts together, so this is a way for a big unwieldy organization to make sure that if there's a solution over in one part of the company that we can reach out and make those connections and get that information there.

Internal networking also creates opportunities for reverse flow of information where the younger team members can bring in new knowledge to address an old problem. Perhaps a Generation Y or Millennial employee has found a new technology or solution that was previously non-existent and can address that one issue which made it impossible to achieve the technical goals in the past. Creating an environment conducive to this kind of information sharing (be it company legends or discussions of new possibilities) among employees constitutes the core of tacit knowledge management.

How companies approach knowledge management eventually feeds back into company culture. For example, if a culture uses heavy documentation to document all of the processes explicitly, this carefulness may lead to reduced productivity, reduced innovation, and a slower pace of change. Companies focused on internal networking as a means of knowledge management really valued internal networking, and that was reflected in the company culture. In the words of a Chief Technical Officer:

> Culture really is extraordinarily important, and I've known people that are just really smart people, but   a

big part of our culture is being able to talk to other people and being able to network. If you're not a good networker, you're going to struggle here because it's very much a team sport, and so, you know, if we have the Einstein kind of genius, I don't know if that would really be appreciated here.

While I don't endorse this particular view, it appears that within that particular company's specific cultural context, it makes a sort of "cultural sense," to forgo the documented benefits of selecting higher performing employees. For example, if you boost the performance of your top quartile of performers by 10%, you can improve overall organizational productivity by 7.5%. To achieve the same 7.5% productivity gain with the remaining 75% of performers, you would need to improve their performance by a full 30%! Truly outstanding employees can increase the bottom line by even more, and have demonstrated an increased likelihood of sharing that information—a factor that was was found to account for 73.1% of variability in organizational effectiveness (Yang, 2007).

Employee Engagement

In popular parlance, employee engagement is understood as involving one of two things: either as a specific focus on *employee traits*—which make a particular employee *ideal* regardless of company context—or *formal recognition*, which involves designing an employee recognition program so that there are formal and tangible rewards. A lot of ink has been spilled about employee engagement both in the academic journals and in popular management publications like *Harvard Business Review*. But neither of these views quite captures the phenomenon.

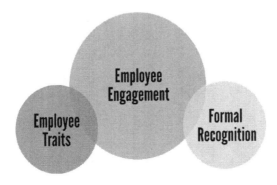

As I talked to leaders in the stellar high performing organizations, I found that they were discussing a third way of employee engagement. What they meant was that there were things which employers do for employees, which serve to engage the employees. These activities had nothing to do with formal recognition—which shy employees hated—and they had nothing to do with some sort of eugenic search for the perfect blonde-haired blue-eyed engaged employee to be identified by the Applicant Tracking System or I/O psychologist.

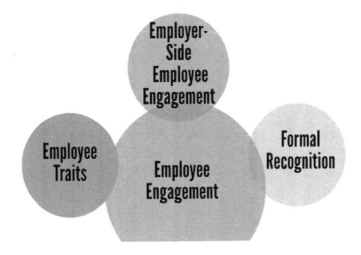

There was a strong recognition in these exemplary firms that employees were not interchangeable, and that not everyone was motivated by the same things. They really strove to understand the employees as individuals, and, to paraphrase what Jack Kennedy said, "Asked what they could do for their employees, not what their employees could do for them."

In a Fortune 500 company's Marketing Manager's experience:

> One of the things that I've found is that some people are very uncomfortable with being recognized in front of a large crowd. So, matching up their desire with how you recognize them is probably more important than having those formal recognition programs in place. I've had open conversations with my employees saying, OK, so let's say you do a great job, how do you want me to recognize you? You want me to send you an email? That's a private thing. Is it would you like to be recognized in front of a large crowd? Some people would rather crawl under a table than be recognized in a large crowd.

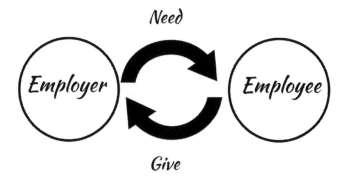

Taken a step further, there was also a strong recognition that the ideal employee at another firm wouldn't necessarily make a great employee in their own company. Instead, there was a view that how an employee fit the culture was a significant factor in employee success. Just as you may not really think that your spouse or a significant other is really *perfect*, as an example of human perfection to be put on a pedestal and admired alongside Michelangelo's David, but instead *perfect for you*, leading companies recognize that there is a substantial difference between the two. A person doesn't have to be perfect in order to be effective, and organizational culture plays a significant role in whether a good individual will be great in a given circumstance or not. Conversely, these firms also acknowledged that great individuals might not live up to their potential if a company failed to support and engage them. Employee engagement is as much about the employer as the employee—and just as no relationship is one-sided, neither is the employment relationship. High performing companies invested in their employee relationship just as they hoped their employees would invest in the company.

Organizational learning from the environment

Ultimately, in many ways, the market environment tends to shape an organization and its culture. Organizational learning—including past experiences and lessons from the market environment—come to shape a company culture over time. Company culture is perhaps just an accretion of experiences, built up over time, and a particular reaction to them.

Just as a pearl is formed from the irritation of external sand entering an oyster, causing the oyster to build a cover of nacre to protect itself, so too, company culture may be a pearl formed through difficult or irritating lessons from the external environment, and the company developing its reactions to the experience in order to survive.

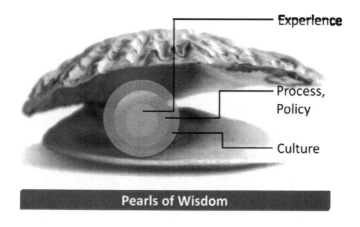

Pearls of Wisdom

Several executives at a manufacturing firm were quick to point out how a troubled time in their company history several decades ago shaped their culture today. At the time, the firm had been purchasing jets and constructing new office buildings and flying high on Wall Street. But the economy suddenly slowed, and its seasonal products were purchased at a much slower rate. The inventory started piling up. The CEO at the time said, "There's never going to be a time when our products aren't needed," and despite the high inventory, made a decision to keep producing, in order to squeeze cost out of the product by running the factories at full capacity. More units of the product piled up. But for a second year, the weather didn't cooperate. This was unprecedented, and had never happened before in the company's long history. But the company was still spending cash in order to manufacture and stay in business. By this time, the bank was getting worried and initiated discussions to pull financing. The manufacturer managed to negotiate for more time. The CEO doubled-down on his strategy, "The weather has always cooperated. It's something like a million-to-one odds that it won't cooperate. We're going to be able to move product, because we'll have pent-up demand since customers haven't been buying for two years." Famous last words! That year, the weather didn't cooperate again and more of the product piled up in warehouses.

At the time, there was no reason the company shouldn't have gone bankrupt. The company books were dismal, inventory was high, and the cash flow was drawn to a trickle. But somehow, the company employees had developed close relationships with the lenders, and managed to convince the bank not to pull financing. Because the bankers liked them, they gave them a little more leeway than they otherwise would have—and maybe even objectively should have—and that made all of the difference. Ultimately, it was only the employee relationships that saved the company from bankruptcy.

According to the company's Senior Organizational Development Manager:

> There was a point in history where the organization went through a very difficult time, a couple decades ago

and almost went under, and the president made a very good decision to define what he thought the corporate values were and really diffuse those throughout the organization. It's become a strong foundation of this organization that is woven into so many different things, so we're driven by our people values.

It was from this harsh lesson from the market that the manufacturing company decided to focus on its employees as a source of value. From the irritant emerged the pearl.

A less drastic story, but no less compelling, was told to me by the Director of Business Development at a financial services firm. His company and the way it did business changed dramatically in the wake of the 2009 financial crisis. In the aftermath of what Blackstone Group's CEO Stephen Schwartzman reported to be a 45% destruction of global wealth, the external conditions of the financial meltdown also had internal repercussions for the financial services firm; indeed, the conditions led the company to reconsider its priorities, from balancing internal employee demands and customer service, to a strategy that involved solely focusing on clients.

> A lot of bad press, a lot of really bad decisions, and a few really bad dogs cost the industry. Take an economic downturn and the spotlight was hot and heavy and the microscopes were on every policy and procedure, and it really forced the industry as a whole to become much more transparent; the majority of it was always 'we're client first.' But now the business is regulated in a way that it is just a client first business; what's right for the client.

What successful firms demonstrated was that there was no such thing as a bad experience, except for the experience that a company failed to learn from.

Consequences

Understanding that company culture influences the organizational learning process—what approaches a company takes, what approaches they avoid, and how they do things—is important. Much of what counts as culture, and serves as a way of being, is actually wisdom built up through experiences. It is important to honor those experiences, which are valid and valuable.

A lot of the chaos that occurs in organizations can be attributed to change efforts that don't fit a company's culture. Strategies that don't fit, organizational development tools that assume too much, learning interventions that stretch employees to the point of breaking, processes that are too intense, approaches to documentation that don't fit the context—all of these negative things occur when somebody fails to take organizational culture into account.

When we understand the big picture of how an organization works, we can understand what actions we should take in a given circumstance, and what our constraints are. No matter how exciting a change is employees who have seen a similar circumstance go wrong aren't likely to support it. And indeed, they may have good reasons to resist. If you look at culture as a pearl—built up, solidified wisdom that emerges from layers of hard experience—then it makes sense to honor those lessons learned. Too often, new leaders enter an organization with an agenda for change—and change for change's sake rather than any compelling business reason. If you are to effect real change, you must entwine both knowing and doing and ask, "Knowing what I know now, should I act differently?" (Weick, 1969).

As a result of applying these findings to your company, you will be able to:

- Make decisions based on data rather than theory
- Better control decision processes
- Reduce blind spots in competitive strategy that impact performance
- More clearly manage risk
- Make wiser use of training and development budgets
- Introduce more effective product and market innovations

Exercise II: Succinctly Defining Our Company Culture

Use the **Guiding Questions** to come up with a **Succinct Definition** of your company culture.

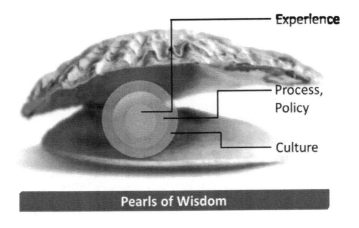

Guiding Questions

Where have we been and what did we learn?

1) What were the key, defining moments in our company's history?

2) What did we learn from these moments?

3) What other lessons might we have taken from these moments in our company's history?

How do we __DO__ business?

1) What is our client focus?

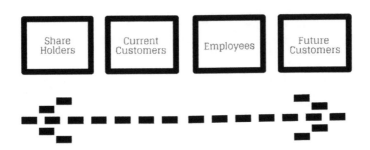

| Share Holders | Current Customers | Employees | Future Customers |

Short Term   Long Term

2) What type of growth strategy are we pursuing?

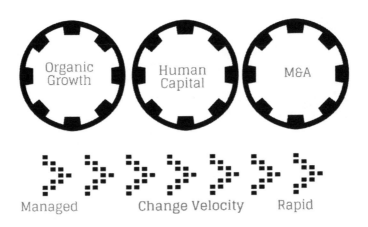

Organic Growth   Human Capital   M&A

Managed   Change Velocity   Rapid

3) How do we manage knowledge?

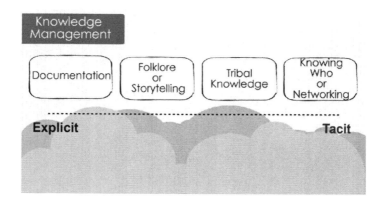

4) How do we engage our employees?

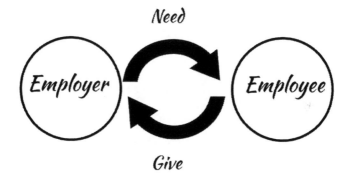

Succinct Definition

Choose 5-10 words to write a succinct definition of your company culture.

```
┌─────────────────────────────────────────────┐
│                                             │
│                                             │
│                                             │
│                                             │
│                                             │
│                                             │
│                                             │
│                                             │
│                                             │
└─────────────────────────────────────────────┘
```

Review

Once you have done this, your work still isn't finished. Now consider: would managers in other groups or employees agree with this definition? If not, take this opportunity to revise. What we are looking for is not a description of the way we *wish it would be*, but *how people feel it really is*, in order to serve as an accurate starting point or "ground zero" for discussions and strategizing. Once you have succinctly defined your culture, it will become much easier to determine strategy, tactics, and implementation.

3 | Being: Culture Is A Way of Being

"Organizations, like people, are creatures of habit. For organizations, the existing habits are norms, systems, procedures, written and unwritten rules— *'the way we do things around here'*"- R.H. Waterman

Galileo questioned the idea of the geocentric universe, with the world at its center, and mankind as the center of all things, as Aristotle had posited. Because of his questioning, he was met with strong opposition from both astronomers and the clergy who had come to believe that the earth was the center of the universe. Since people had developed particular habits of the mind, and long taken the notion of a geocentric universe for granted, it was difficult for them to understand a sun-centered system that was antithetical to the universe that they knew. It was not simply that Galileo questioned whether the sun orbited the earth—which was the tip of the iceberg— but all of the social implications, norms, scripture, and philosophy based upon this map of the universe—that made Galileo's assertion heretical. It was not simply that Galileo questioned an idea academically; it was that Galileo challenged people's very notions of *the way things were* and of *the way we do things around here*. It wasn't simply that he was criticizing an idea—he was criticizing *them*.

Galileo questioned people's *a priori* assumptions, the first principles that people saw as self-evident and took for granted. Naturally, it made people uncomfortable. To put it into context, imagine how you might respond if someone new came into your office and told you how to do your work...

And yet, this is often what makes company culture change so difficult. External consultants or new executives often come in and simply announce that a company will do things differently—starting today and continuing from now on. This is difficult and often garners pushback. Whatever good that a company has built, whatever results a company has achieved in the past, whatever lessons a company has learned from its environment, are simply pushed aside for an unproven "new." It is no wonder that corporate change is rarely successful— with 70% of organizational change efforts failing outright, and up to 90% of mergers and acquisitions failing to take root.

If Galileo had reflected on his experiences, he may have learned that change is most likely to take root when it matches the culture, when it recognizes and acknowledges past contributions, and when it doesn't threaten people's *way of being*. Perhaps if he had framed his realization differently, Galileo would have been more successful in getting his message across. While culture is often intangible, it is an immensely important thing to account for. In many ways, culture bounds what is deemed possible. Contradict the culture, and you are almost certain to get burned.

Nevertheless, culture is often invisible. In my experience, asking people to describe their company culture is a lot like asking a goldfish to describe the inside of its fishbowl. Employees may have a difficult time formulating their thoughts to describe a company's culture simply because "that's just the way we do things around here." It is so much a part of the surrounding atmosphere that we sometimes forget that it's even there. It is only when people oppose the culture that its importance becomes evident—it's like when you touch an invisible dog fence, and get a shock. Culture is a powerful force, which we rarely stop to think about.

In the words of a Chief Technical Officer:

> The culture is such a critical part of the company, and if you don't get that piece you're going to struggle here. Our company has traditionally hired people out of college, and then they learn about the culture that way, so it's second nature to them. Really, I think it does have a very big impact, so the way that I would describe our culture is that we tend to hire really good people, we tend to hire people that are pretty social, and like to interact with people in a nice Midwest kind of way.

Indeed, a company's culture permeates everything—from the way that work is done, to how often you have to seek approval to complete work, to how often people drink coffee (or soda!). It's embedded in things as ephemeral as whether the office is abuzz with chatter or is so silent, you can almost hear crickets. Culture is fluid, but it's like blood coursing through the veins of the company, flowing through everything, and making it come alive. Culture is what makes working in one company different from another within the same industry. In the words of a production manager in an industry that was devastated by layoffs:

> The company culture here is one of strong commitments and no layoffs so throughout the whole last several years, we've moved people around.

This made the firm a very different place to work than other companies in the same industry. Company culture guides a company's reaction to external events—which may lead a firm to do things differently.

In some sense, company culture can be seen as a form of competitive advantage. A previous study of 759 companies suggested that corporate culture is a much greater driver of innovation than labor, capital, government, or national culture (Tellis, Prabhu, & Chandy, 2009). This suggests that no matter how difficult company culture is to pin down, it is important to get some sense of it since company culture represents a starting point for organizations, from which all actions flow.

The way of being in a company changes a company's approach to the activities it is involved in doing, and the approaches to action which are believed to be reasonable ways of doing things, versus approaches which may be deemed less acceptable. For example, at some firms it is an absolute given that if a deadline is looming for customer delivery, and an employee has his or her vacation scheduled, that that vacation will be cancelled immediately. In the words of one software trainer:

> It's frustrating with some of these projects. They want me to go out and teach these people the software; well, either the software's not ready or they had to pull it back, and one time they even got me off the airplane before I took off (for vacation).

At other companies, prioritizing customers to this extreme would be unthinkable, since the company culture might prioritize employee satisfaction, which was particularly true in many family-owned or employee-owned companies. An employee health and safety professional at a manufacturing firm described the practical results of his company's employee-oriented focus:

> There's an employee club here that uses money, essentially from our company and purchases lunches and does little things on pretty much a monthly basis,

and the guys have just grown to expect that it is going to continue. And you say, 'Man, that doesn't happen elsewhere.' And we do an annual lunch, and give away little prizes and things like that. Last year budgeting was tough, so we did it here as opposed to off-site and there were complaints. They could have said, 'we could just scrap it altogether and save 5 or 10 thousand dollars if you're not going to appreciate it,' but they didn't. So I think there's definitely a focus on employees.

The difference between a situation being absolutely unthinkable and an absolute given is essentially a difference in culture. When attempting to plan a change—whether that is a change to process, policy, or strategy—understanding the company culture and common mental models of the way things work is tremendously helpful.

Unfortunately, strategy is often planned by consultants and leaders with a close attention to financials, but little attention to company culture. In most cases, this is a mistake, since employees are called upon to enact change, and are unlikely to carry out change if it contradicts the company's core beliefs and values. The more that a change contradicts ingrained systems and ways of doing things, the more resistance leaders are likely to encounter. Blaming the employees for being stubborn does nothing to mitigate the resistance, since those resisting the change have obviously seen successful outcomes from those exact behaviors in the past. In some cases, employees may be resistant to a change primarily because it involves changing key ways of doing things that a company has learned from operating in its niche environment.

Essentially, there exist six main causes of organizational resistance.

6 Causes of Organizational Resistance

Success Bias

The skills which got a company to this point won't usually get a company to the next level. A few decades ago, Smith-Corona was one of the best typewriter manufacturers in the world. And before the advent of personal computers, laptops, and mobile devices, typewriters were big business. As part of its strategy, Smith-Corona had always focused on quality. Their engineers believed that if they could make typewriters more indestructible, if they could add even more useful features, and if they could keep finding ways to add quality to their product, customers would keep on coming. Quality had been a recipe for success. So while IBM began taking over the market by focusing on computers, Smith-Corona's engineers decided that computers weren't needed—better quality typewriters were the future. We all know how that turned out. In retrospect, it's easy to see what happened—but in the heat of battle, it's often difficult to abandon a tried and true recipe for success in favor of an unknown one.

If failures are lessons that lead to success, company successes can be costly lessons that eventually lead to failure. A Chinese Zen folktale captures this phenomenon perfectly: Once there was a Chinese farmer who worked the land with his son. One day, their horse ran away. The farmers' neighbors came to commiserate, saying, "How unfortunate!" The farmer replied, "Maybe yes, maybe no." A few days later, the horse returned, followed by an entire herd of wild horses. When the neighbors of the village heard the news, they came to help celebrate. "What good luck!" they exclaimed. The farmer remained calm and replied, "Maybe yes, maybe no." Later, when the farmers' son fell and broke his leg while trying to tame a wild horse, the neighbors cried, "How sad for you." The farmer again took it in stride, and replied, "Maybe yes, maybe no." Shortly thereafter, the emperor began drafting the young men of the village to fight a war. The son was not drafted because of his broken leg. "What good luck!" the neighbors said. "Maybe yes, maybe no," the farmer replied.

As the folktale puts it, sometimes unfortunate events can be fortunate, and the fortunate events can be truly unfortunate. This is no less true for companies, where success bias can inhibit learning the new lessons which will lead to future successes.

Defensive Routines

Defensive routines are a common reaction to an embarrassing situation or an assumption that things just won't change. At a high tech firm, a sales manager recounted just such an incident. He knew first hand from customers that a software feature was broken in their most popular commercial product line. Customers had been calling his mobile phone at all hours for weeks to tell him about it. While he tried to soothe their complaints the best that he could, he also knew that the R&D engineers were swamped with a high-priority project, which the CEO touted as "the next big thing." There had been a large "product launch" celebration that investors had been on hand to witness. All of the team meetings over the past few months had focused on how the new project was running. So when the CEO approached the sales manager and asked him directly how things were going, he decided not to tell the CEO about the broken feature on the old product. Besides, the head of R&D was an unpleasant man whom he preferred to avoid as much as possible, given their past disagreements over resources and work outputs. Ultimately, the sales manager figured it was better to keep things under his hat, until the R&D engineers had a little more time and leeway to fix the problem, even if it meant leaving his customers hanging.

This defensive routine occurred because the sales manager hesitated to put himself in an uncomfortable spot—especially knowing that things may not change, even if he did make the announcement. Would it have been better for customers if the company had quickly fixed the underlying issues? Of course—and if the issue lingers for too long, it will almost certainly do damage to the company's reputation, which is even more difficult to repair than the original problem. Although avoiding dealing with a situation directly prevents direct conflict, it almost always comes at the cost of tension and anxiety, merely delaying or postponing the conflict until a later date.

Situations where people avoid raising the alarm, procrastinate, engage the group in "paralysis by analysis," or provide mixed messages to spare people's feelings (for example, saying, "I'll think about it," when the answer is really just "no,") are defensive routines to avoid hurting the team. But by failing to be more direct with issues or challenges, the organization often suffers. Delays in information that occur as a result of an individual's attempt to save face or spare feelings often have disastrous consequences—as damaged products go out the door, bugs remain unfixed, needed changes are left unmade, and uncomfortable announcements left unsaid.

Cognitive Rigidities

Simply put, an organization may have trouble "thinking outside of the box." If team members automatically reject ideas, because "that's not the way we do things here," without asking why, that team may be experiencing cognitive rigidities. These habits of action typically have their roots in habits of thought. Examining why things are done in a particular way may help to break down rigid habits of thought which may have outlived their usefulness.

Just as stretching is useful, and helps to make you more flexible, companies that don't stretch themselves as part of a regular practice—by questioning why they do what they do, by asking if there might be other more effective ways of doing things, or by simply changing up the order in which they approach work in order to get their creative juices flowing— may risk becoming stiff and inflexible. As markets experience more turbulence—that is, unexpected change, rapid product turnover, increased global competition, and sudden shifts in consumer demand—it is becoming increasingly important to be flexible and agile. No company wants to remain stiff and rigid in a rapidly changing world.

Departmental Siloing

Even in this era of increased open space floor plans and falling cubicle walls, departmental siloing frequently occurs. This is because departmental siloing has more to do with *emotional barriers* than *physical ones*. Leaders who butt heads with each other or who have conflicting visions can drive a wedge between teams, creating a structural insularity that is hard to overcome. A training manager in a Fortune 500 described her company this way:

> There are a multitude of divisions, and each of these divisions report to its own VP, which again, if you

carve it out, would be the president of a very large company on its own. And the way it works is very siloed.

Many times, a company's departments are arranged like eggs in a carton—neatly self-contained in their shells, not bumping into others. Yet, if organizations are to truly experience success, groups must get outside of their shells and mix. Just as you may have to crack a few eggs to make an omelet, you sometimes have to mix the groups to make a company. Organizations depend upon synergy between groups in order to exceed the value produced by any teams or individuals.

A Training Manager at a high tech software company described her experience with this process:

> You've kind of caught me at a unique time period. We are going from working in our own individual silos *per se*, and we are moving to a very collaborative environment. So they're building out a space for us that is non-office. Most of us will no longer have an office. So it will be an open space model and we will have a backlog of projects or things that we'll be working on, and we will be placed on those projects in two week sprints so it's more of an agile world.

Groupthink

While there are many kinds of conflict, several of which are harmful, process conflict is often beneficial to running an organization more smoothly. For a person to be willing to open him or herself up to possible ridicule in a company meeting is a wonderful gift which speaks to the success of the organization in engendering trust. Unfortunately, in many company settings, the emphasis placed on "fitting in the corporate culture" pretty much puts an end to any possibility that employees are going to step out of line and risk being branded a heretic in order to share a wild idea that could revolutionize your market. The personal risk is too great, while the reward for doing so is uncertain at best.

When companies hire for "cultural fit," they have already screened out a lot of contrarians who might have innovated by taking a different perspective or tact than the members already on board. And if those who have been hired get the message that they need to go along to get along, why risk their job by stepping out of line? Such hiring practices therefore may increase an organization's risk of groupthink both directly through the screening process, and indirectly through the tacit messages which the company conveys to its employees through endorsing the practice.

But in companies where increasingly complex products are made which depend upon many players' skill sets for success, it's not enough to just think differently—the person who is thinking differently must also share their idea. The single best way to ensure that a company isn't blindsided by a change in the market that it just didn't see is to allow, and even encourage, process conflict—whether that entails thinking through each of the many ways to a solution, brainstorming new plans, or viewing risk and challenges differently.

Contradicting Company Culture

Nothing adds more sudden conflict into a company culture than adding another company culture into the mix. No wonder that 80% of mergers and acquisitions—in which two distinct company cultures to come together—fail! (Ashkenas, 2013).

Gerald Levin, the former CEO of Time Warner, helped to engineer a merger between Time and Warner

Communications. This merger was generally seen as a bad deal for Time. In an effort to compensate for the poorly advised merger with Warner Communications, Levin sold Time Warner to AOL in 2001 in one of the most catastrophic mergers in the history of American business, a deal which lost $200 billion in shareholder's money. But why the failure? Mixing company cultures. The differences were enormous, and left unaddressed, became insurmountable.

When two merging firm's contradictory assumptions shape the differing approaches to the areas of knowledge management, client focus, strategy for growth, and engagement, the impact on a firm's actions are enormous. Processes can become distorted and misunderstandings over job titles and role responsibilities can cause challenges.

A Manufacturing Engineer provided an example:

> An engineer in one area doesn't necessarily do the same things as what an engineer in the other areas do. There's a lot of overlap, you can have a lot of common parts, but not in others, and an example of that would be in a machine shop where the individual engineers do the quoting on new parts. So they would get a new drawing from corporate and they would say well, "I'm going to run it on this machine, and I can do it at this rate, and because of that, the cost would be this," and we have to bid our work. In the area that I work in, in tooled stampings, I don't do the quoting. Our tooling engineer does the quoting and there's a good reason for it, and the reason is that in tool stampings, the quoting is so determined by the tooling, that if you don't know what the tooling will be, you don't know how to quote it and so our tooling engineer quotes it. Kind of what I'm getting at, though, is that there are some slight differences,

but yet we all basically have the same job description. So we've been talking about that recently, and it leads to some confusion. Even amongst ourselves, we make assumptions that well, "this should be your job because it's my job; it's part of my job, so it should be part of your job," the other guy will go, "no, I don't do that," so it could be better defined.

Even where roles are clearly defined, sudden expansion often comes at a cost of knowing who to go to for help, and what the right policy is. Duplicate policies for events that are less than regular occurrences may fly under the company radar for quite some time—only surfacing when a conflict arises. Since few companies set expiry dates on policies to ensure that there is a regular review, document repositories can become cluttered recycling bins of outdated and self-contradictory policies fairly quickly.

Differences in mental models about what the right thing to do, how one should contribute to one's company's success, what sorts of issues one has free reign to make decisions on, and what level of risk is acceptable, often leads to rifts between old and integrating companies. These sorts of differences may lead to interpersonal conflicts, which surface when roles clash. Many employees with radically different lifestyles, opinions, preferences, and political persuasions can work seamlessly together as long as the work is clearly defined and their work pieces fit together as a whole. I have seen workplaces where "frat boy" types worked side by side with self-described "farm kids," and classical music-loving academics to achieve great results. These employees ranged from introverted to extroverted, and came from locations around the U.S. and the world—from East to West Coast, Midwest, and South, to India, China, Malaysia, and Ghana. They came from different generations, ranging from Baby Boomers to Millennials. Despite their rich perspectives and vast array of life experiences, it was no matter. None of these rather superficial differences come to matter unless there is a root conflict in the work itself. Then, like Pandora opening her box, all of the superficial clutter flies out—encircling the organization—and often surfacing as an excuse. "I can't work with this guy. He's such a farm boy, always meddling in everything, never thinking through the outcomes." Yet, this personal conflict is essentially a lie—something we add to our stack of evidence to bolster our narrative of "good vs. evil" and why things aren't getting done. Personal conflict is a mere symptom of the real problem. Fix the root cause, and you fix the problem—and its symptoms as well.

Cultures persist over time, and the imprint of employees' ways of doing things lasts long after they leave the organization. Which is why, for the most part, mergers fail. When you have clashing cultures, each leaving their imprint, it causes conflict and confusion. Yet despite an astonishing failure rate related to mergers and acquisitions, and difficult if not insurmountable challenges, in bringing vastly different cultures together, mergers and acquisitions continue to be a favored way for larger companies to grow and innovate— mainly because it is perceived as cheaper and "less risky" than building innovation from the ground up which would require potentially funding failures as well as successes. Shareholders often promote mergers as a singular method for innovation since it occurs over the short-term time frame that they view the business world through.

Occasionally, acquisitions are purchased not so much for the intellectual property of a firm, but to help acquiring companies to penetrate a market more quickly. In these instances, acquisitions are not for innovation as much as to use the acquisition as a vehicle for conveying and transmitting one's own products into new markets. In the words of a Chief Technical Officer:

[We] grow through mergers and acquisitions but primarily, more in a sense of enabling acquisitions to penetrate a market more quickly; to get a distribution network more readily, to penetrate a country because of trademarks or things like that; prior earning that the local population might have with that company that can serve as a platform that we can pull in. So that's where the mergers and acquisitions piece comes in.

Then, too, there are sometimes situations where market rewards can be reaped from branding alone simply slapping a brand name label on a particular product may increase its value exponentially in many markets, without doing a thing to change the underlying product. Where opportunities to profit by purchasing and rebranding exist, it is difficult to resist the temptation of acquisitions.

If M&A is a primary driver of a company's growth and innovation, it is best to examine corporate culture first—both that of the company, and that of the company to be merged. Arguably, a cultural assessment may be a far better long-term predictor of the success of an M&A than financial indicants, which tend to be shorter-term in focus. While the numbers may make sense, the assumptions of the people may not be shared—leading to trouble down the line.

When assessing a potential acquisition, it is best to assume that what you see is what you get. No acquiring company is likely to be able to change the acquired firm too much after the acquisition, just as no bride is able to "change" the groom after the wedding. So buyer beware! Know what you have, know what you're getting into, and know own company's capacity to deal with it. Anything else is just fantasy, no matter how pretty or profitable the daydream.

Exercise III: Digging into Resistance to Change

When processes change, it sometimes requires a change in mental models or mindset as well as changing the underlying process itself. Communicating this change and why the change is required now may help ease the transition, since ways of doing things are intimately connected with company culture.

Since change is a constant in any living company, it is often necessary to pinpoint the actual *root cause* of resistance, in order to better address why the change is encountering resistance. To do so, ask the following questions:

- **Are you encountering resistance to change?**

- **If so, is the resistance coming from a handful of vocal people, or is it distributed more broadly?**

- **Can you pinpoint the cause of organizational resistance? (See 6 causes of organizational resistance)**

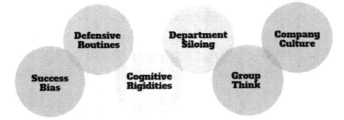

6 Causes of Organizational Resistance

Defensive routines

- Is the issue personally embarrassing?

- Why don't you think things will change?

Success Bias

- Have we been successful in this area in the past?

- What would happen if we approached things completely differently?

Departmental Siloing

- Why do we feel that the situation is "us" versus "them"?

- Are the departments being rewarded for different outcomes?

- How do department leaders' personalities shape each of the groups?

Cognitive Rigidities

- Why are things done this way?

- What were the reasons behind it?

- Are these reasons still relevant now?

- What has changed since we put the original process or policy in place?

Groupthink and reduced process conflict

- Is "getting along with others" rewarded?

- Are there ways in which we could better reward innovative behaviors?

Contradicting Company Culture

- Do the new processes or changes conflict with company culture?

- Is there a way to take a gradual approach to slowly change in order to adapt to the proposed change?

- Is the change really necessary? How necessary is it to make this particular change now? What would happen if this change were not made?

4 | Doing: Who is it all for?

"No man can serve two masters." -Matthew 6:24

Seeing a clear path of stars to the outer reaches of the universe is magnificent and breath-taking. But just as Galileo was eventually forced to invert the lens of his telescope to see the world in which he lived in closer detail—creating a microscope—so, too, must businesses turn their focus within to drive better understanding and improve this-worldly results.

By looking *within* the company, and finding the levers of change which are within the firm's reach and which are controllable— rather than imagining how to control each and every market competitor, supplier, emerging small business, and customer in the entire market web (as most current strategic models grandly do)—it becomes easier to take action. Instead of taking a prescientific understanding, and cursing the gods for creating the difficult market conditions, you can understand and change your own company's actions to improve the company's results. Of all the internal factors that are important to understand, first and foremost, a company must understand who their business is ultimately for, since no company can fully serve two masters.

When you ask almost any employee who it's all for, and why a company does what it does, the employees reflexively tell you, "It's for our customers." Sayings like, "The customer is always right," imply that companies focus solely on those who buy their products. But if you probe employees further and ask, "If a hard decision has to be made, and not everyone can get what they want, who would get what they want?" they turn the lens of the microscope to focus within the company. Suddenly, their answer is more reflective, deeper, and often starkly different. Depending on the company, the customer isn't always going to get what they want, no matter the cost. Many leading companies do very well, but may ultimately favor *shareholders, end users,* or even *employees* over *customer needs or desires.*

There are times when you can't please everyone. It's those times which are the most revealing since they demonstrate *who* and *what* a company really values. These values are what are non-negotiable and show who a company really is at its core. The segment who gets what they want has the most power over a company's culture and ultimately, future. The primary customer served is the *de facto* master of the company—above CEO's, above power structures, and above any rhetoric of company values.

Who the ultimate master of the company is tends to shape the company's culture, what actions are deemed appropriate, and in what strategic direction the company is eventually heading. When stakeholders' interests conflict, one of the groups almost always emerges as the ultimate victor; taking the lion's share of the mindshare, resources, time, and commitments. Even in resource constrained times or under poor market conditions, primary customers tend to get what they want. When the rubber hits the road, not everyone's opinion is equal or as impactful. If a company ultimately favors its employees, and wants to do right by them, the shareholders clamoring for pay cuts aren't going to get the returns they want and that will be the end of it. But if a company favors its shareholders' satisfaction over all else, employee tenure is likely plummet as the company seeks to streamline services, reduce costs, increase workloads, and cut pay in order to achieve shareholders' targets for an ideal percent of return.

This difference in primary customer focus serves to differentiate companies, even within the same competitive industry. There is a different "feel" to a company that is *employee-focused* rather than *shareholder-focused*. This qualitative difference may be difficult to articulate, but is immediately noticeable when you step into a firm.

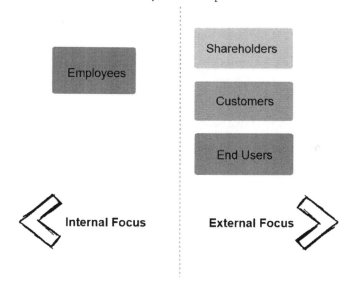

There exist four ultimate corporate orientations— *shareholder focused, customer focused, employee focused,* and *end-user focused.* These orientations range from internally focused to externally focused, although the majority of the orientations are externally focused. Depending on who these ultimate "masters" are, with their varying interests, companies inevitably aspire to obtain different end results—for *profit*, *people*, or *planet*. These results, naturally, occur over different timelines—whether as short term as next quarter, or as long-term as decades.

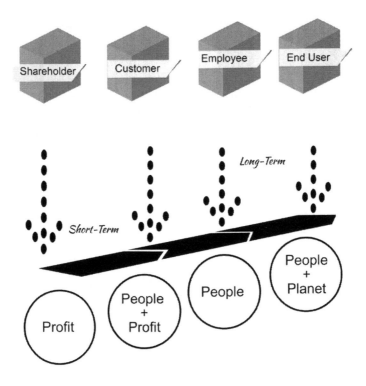

Shareholder-Focused

Shareholders may be a form of customer, but they have uniquely different interests than the usual customers who simply buy a product or service. While customers might desire wide a product selection, which could potentially eat into company profits, shareholders are most interested in their returns. So while a customer may want or demand many product lines be offered, shareholders may be just as vocal in their recommendation that unprofitable or merely marginally profitable product lines be discontinued. In many cases, the interests of shareholders and customers may widely diverge.

Companies that are shareholder-focused may see immediate returns reflected in share prices and efficiency measures, but often lack employee retention or engagement. Knowledge sharing may be impeded in such environments due to the difficult company-employee relationship that results from such pressures. In such environments, employees may feel it necessary to hoard their knowledge, since their knowledge or ability has a tangible value (i.e., they are being paid for it, and do not work for free), and this asset keeps them from being replaced. When decisions are made based on the bottom line, employees often fear being replaced by newer, cheaper, employees, increased process improvements, outsourcing—or even automation.

Companies driven by shareholder value often try to squeeze value for shareholders at almost any cost. In some instances this manifests in a higher level of concentration on high-performers. In the words of a customer services trainer:

> Sometimes I get the idea that we make decisions in our company and it all has to do with the bottom line. For instance, there's a group of employees that are very high producers and we cater to that group, so they have their own special help desk to call into, they get other perks, they get a trip every year, they get higher pay out and they just get these extra added bonuses even to the point that when we want to go out and train people on some new software, we're told, "You have to train to this group first before you train other people because those are the guys that make the most money."

Many companies try to squeeze shareholder value through process improvements. Process improvements frequently go hand-in-hand with delivering value for shareholders. Yet, a narrow focus on short-term measures—such as ROI (return on investment), cost savings, and efficiency-sometimes leads to a neglect of longer-term planning or a focus on employee retention. In the words of a Manufacturing Trainer:

> The company focuses more on efficiency. For example, as far as I know, there's no succession planning, there is no mentoring for the sake of progression, or growth and so forth, and there is no company-wide human capital strategy that I can speak to...

In companies where shareholder value is the ultimate yardstick of success, employee satisfaction, retention, or training isn't likely to matter as much. Executive compensation packages and rewards are based on generating shareholder value. When hard decisions have to be made impacting today's bottom line, the longer term value generated by employee satisfaction or continuity isn't likely to take precedence over the immediate tangible returns. As a result, shareholder focused companies tend to favor a short-term time orientation—looking at today, tomorrow, this quarter, and next quarter—rather than three years, five years, or decades down the line.

Customer-Focused

Customer focused companies often seek to build long-term customer loyalty through providing good service and products to customers. Customer-focused companies are frequently profitable, but their actions may not always be pleasing to investors. For example, customer-focused companies might invest in orphan drugs for rare medical conditions simply because customers need them, or provide services or delivery to rural areas which don't have the best profit margins simply because it's the right thing to do for the customer. These actions might not be the most convenient, or the most profitable in the very short-term, but can contribute to customer satisfaction, and over time, customer loyalty. Where the costs to acquire a new customer are high, retaining customers makes sense.

In the words of a software industry employee:

> I can't speak for the executive suite, but I think that by and large the people that I work with are pretty focused on customers. Especially as the world moves towards people [continually] using online services, if the service goes down, you know there's someone here who's on the hook on the beeper call and it could be two in the morning. It's sort of like you're never away from your work; you just never know when a problem could come up. People are always on call. I think all of that's in service of the customer. There's never a time when five o'clock on a Friday [when] we're just going to shut down until 9 o'clock on Monday morning.

Being *always on call* and having a strong support staff may not generate a lot of profit in the short term. Labor costs money. But by providing that convenience, and ensuring that customers get what they need; these firms may slowly but surely expand their share of the market.

In some companies, this focus on customers can be so radical that it can overrule not only what employees want, but even what the CEO wants to develop strategically.

In the words of a high tech firm's Director:

> At the end of the day, when you're an engineering manufacturing company, you're providing for what the *end users* want. So just because our CEO thinks it's a great idea doesn't mean we're going to build it if there's no customer requirement.

This, unfortunately, can also be a danger. An extreme customer focus—zeroing in on exactly what the customer wants right now—can lead to some myopia in developing innovations since customers don't always know exactly what they want, but may *know it when they see it*—perhaps in a competitors' product. And the time that products take to develop from bench to market is frequently a long process. Often, very customer-focused companies may be a step or two behind the cutting edge, waiting for other firms to "test out" innovative ideas and iron out the details, before they apply them to their own products.

Employee-Focused

Many knowledge-intensive and service-oriented firms focus strongly on employees, not as an end in itself, but as a means of better serving customers. In the words of a manufacturing company's Marketing employee, this reflects an understanding that:

> The result is what is valued, but it's understood that the people get you there.

The employee-focused orientation is a longer-term strategy. It requires time to carry it out and deliver results. You can't build an employee-focused company overnight or in one or two quarters and expect profits. It requires trust, investment in people including benefits, training, and occasional time off. Employee focused companies often have an edge in knowledge sharing, since employees recognize that if they share their particular approach to completing work with others, it won't jeopardize their job. Instead, it may build their reputation and free them to work on something even more exciting.

In the words of a Vice President of a manufacturing company:

> We didn't lay anyone off, I mean, we're right in the midst of a recession, and unlike any of our competitors, we didn't lay anybody off, we didn't close plants, we didn't reduce any benefits.

Such companies often place strong values on their people and their company cultures, and tend to avoid drastic changes such as mergers and acquisitions. Instead, the strategy is a much slower, but sustained growth. In employee-focused companies, it is believed that by valuing employees, these happy employees will better serve customers. With lower turnover rates, and longer-term tenures for employees, these employees may be able to better build lasting relationships with customers, and develop a rapport. By building meaningful relationships with customers, these firms may be better able to understand customer needs—even latent needs which customers may not think to share with the competitors. These insights may ultimately serve as a form of competitive advantage for a firm.

In the words of a Manufacturing Supervisor:

> We really do focus on our employees, to make sure they have all the tools they need, not just hand tools or anything like that but knowledge-based tools, to meet the needs of our customers.

Well-regarded employees who aren't worried about the security of their jobs may be encouraged to provide stronger service to customers. In the words of a Chief Technical Officer:

> Customers are required, but employees are required to deliver on that and if you're not taking care of your employees, ultimately that's going to cause problems from a business continuity standpoint, which is going to be reflected in your service to your customers... Really, employees are our greatest asset.

This focus on employees in order to serve customers is a proven recipe for success. Costco, for example, focuses on employees and customers. Employees are among some of the industry's best-paid—but also most productive—workers. As a result, Costco currently trades at 23 times its anticipated earnings—compared to 12-13 times for Target and Walmart. Despite this obvious value, investors complain that Costco gives its employees "too good of a deal" and that profits could be higher if the store raised prices or cut employee salaries and benefits. Yet, by focusing on the long-term loyalty, rather than short-term profits, Costco has built solid value. It might not please shareholders, but shareholders aren't Costco's focus; employees in service of customers ultimately drive the business.

End-User focused

Not all companies simply focus on current customers. In high tech spaces, current customers often constitute just a tiny fraction of the ultimate market share that these companies hope to capture. Moreover, early adopters often have unique traits and preferences that are dramatically *different from* those of the broader public. For example, the early adopters of a new software may have higher technological skills than the average computer user, may be more willing to accept glitches or crashes, and have higher need for the product. To the extent that early adopters are different from the ultimate customer base that the company hopes to serve, the company may have to adjust its product offering and approach in order to better serve the ultimate end-users.

In the words of a Director:

> My first week, I had a meeting with sales, and the head of sales was kind of asking about tens of millions of dollars or whatever it was, to photograph the forest in Finland from a satellite. And I forget what the money was, but it was just a big spend to photograph the satellite so that we could put it onto maps. And the question around that was that it was a huge amount of money to spend and there's no value, but I think it's one of the things where our founders would say but that it makes it a better product. It's the place to go for everything like that and it starts to build the reputation that we're not nickling and diming around.

To a shareholder-oriented company, spending money now to photograph a forest in Finland which has no direct correlation to the bottom line, or even to current customers, doesn't make a lot of sense. But to an end-user focused company, it makes all the sense in the world—because such a company is not concerned with *shareholders* or even *current customers*, but about the *end users*, the potential customers who may join the customer base in the future, and the extreme long-term value for everyone in the broader community.

This is a very forward-looking and very inclusive orientation. It focuses not only on the current customers, but the potential, future customers—in short, everyone. While end-user focused companies have a lot in common with companies pursuing Corporate Social Responsibility (CSR) or

Triple Bottom Line thinking—focusing on profits, people, and planet, in order to do well by "doing good," these companies not only walk the talk, but have these ideals embedded in their business DNA.

A lot of companies may use Corporate Social Responsibility programs as a form of marketing—obtaining valuable news coverage in exchange for building new stores to LEED certified standards, or cutting emissions. Doing the math, many of these Corporate Social Responsibility programs cost significantly less than a direct advertising spend would cost for the same amount of press coverage. I doubt this fact has escaped the notice of clever sales and marketing departments.

In Britain, the Advertising Standards Authority has warned consumers that some "green" claims might not be authentic. But even where companies have the proof to back up their claims, they might be driven to do *all the right things* for *all the wrong reasons*. This may seem like an academic argument—for example, who really cares why Coca-Cola is making sure there is clean water, as long as they are? But it does matter. Because when there is a downturn and that shiny Corporate Social Responsibility initiative isn't making money, and doesn't make sense to the culture and logic of the company, it may be among the first things that are cut. Companies which are focused on the end-user aren't likely to cut the things that truly matter to them just because of a rough quarter or an indefinite payoff. Companies which serve the end-user do so because it's their reason for being, and when tough decisions have to be made, they aren't going to violate their company culture.

It is easy to talk the talk, but if there is no basis in the company culture, those fine words won't be put into action. Corporate values should be a real basis in a company's culture and ways of doing things. Anything that conflicts with that very real basis will not last long. A person's behaviors are frequently bounded by culture and experience—where they come from, what's a "norm," and what makes sense under those particular social conditions—why would company's ethical behaviors be any different?

Exercise IV: Defining Our Ultimate Stakeholder

Who is your Ultimate Stakeholder? (If a hard decision had to be made, and not everyone could get what they wanted, who would ultimately get what they want?)

What is the time orientation of serving this stakeholder? (Is it a quarterly orientation or span of decades?)

What are the risks involved in serving this stakeholder?

How can these risks be minimized?

What are the limitations of focusing on this stakeholder?

5 | Becoming: Growth Strategy

"The fault lies not in the stars, dear Brutus, but in ourselves."- William Shakespeare, <u>Julius Caesar</u>

Galileo asserted that a parabola was a *theoretically ideal* trajectory of a *uniformly accelerated projectile* in the *absence of friction* and *other real disturbances*. To translate the jargon, Galileo meant something like, "A parabola is a made-up thing which is in no way practically possible, but it's a tool we use to understand the real world." When you think about it, business strategy is a lot like Galileo's parabola—strategy is an idealized form, which aims to *predict* and *control* a path through industry, but which often overlooks some very real, practical aspects which impinge upon its idealized world. To the extent that reality differs from this ideal, we get discrepancies. Every strategy looks good on paper. It's when you try to implement a strategy or a parabola that you run into trouble. The real world gets in the way.

Strategy is such a loaded term. When you hear the word "strategy," you probably envision a board room filled with executives wearing fancy suits, and possibly meeting with a pricey consultant who bills by the minute, discussing detailed charts and graphs. Such a scene is far removed from the day-to-day activity of business operations and getting things done. Yet, strategy becomes an essential part of a company's operations—even on a daily basis. Strategy isn't simply about coming up with some idealized plan, it's also about putting those words into action and gaining a competitive advantage to win market share over and against competitors.

Employees often tie their practical, tactical work to their understanding of the company's strategy. If this strategy isn't clearly enunciated, employees may end up doing work that is at cross-ends with each other—simply because each group thinks it's carrying out the goals of the company given their particular understanding of the strategy from their particular vantage point. Unclear strategy can be a major source of conflict.

Because of the singular importance of strategy, there are many models that have been developed to explain strategy. Perhaps the most well-known example is SWOT analysis. Classical SWOT analysis was developed by Albert Humphrey in the 1960s at Stanford Research Institute, using data from Fortune 500 companies. Humphrey posited that by specifying the Strengths, Weaknesses, Opportunities, and Threats facing a company that companies would be able to better match their internal company environments to the external competitive environments—leading to a *strategic fit*.

Humphrey's SWOT Analysis Model

Although many business schools today continue to train their MBA students in conducting SWOT analyses, these classic exercises have their limits. Companies conducting SWOT analyses have access to only limited information about competitors who often try to keep key information and sales data a trade secret. In addition, companies usually are only able to identify companies that are direct competitors, of a particular size, which have been well-established in a certain geographic location, who are producing directly comparable products today. When you think about it, it is extremely difficult to identify rising companies that may have started in somebody's garage, particularly if that garage is located in a developing country. In a globalizing market, where there are shrinking start-up costs for many businesses, therefore lowering the barriers to entry, this is a relatively common scenario. Companies that rely on trade secrets rather than patents may not reveal a competitive product until it hits the market and can be reverse engineered, possibly by a shell company paid to make the purchase. Moreover, many SWOT analyses entirely miss the indirect competitors which may become a big deal for a company down the road.

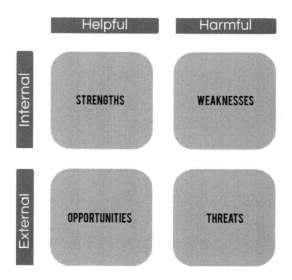

For example, Dillard's department stores are run and controlled by the Dillard family, and hold a chain of about 300 stores. This chain operates in a highly competitive environment which includes Sears, Kohl's, Macy's, and J.C.

Penney. While Dillard's almost certainly saw the other department stores in their SWOT analysis, they appear to have failed to see the rise of online retailer/bookseller Amazon.com's delivery of clothing and shoes as a potential substitute for their department stores.

Or to borrow another example, consumers are beginning to see mobile phones as a product substitute for laptops. Instead of purchasing a new laptop in order to upgrade, they may instead simply select a new mobile phone at a much lower cost. As a mobile phone salesman told recently told me, "I have more memory and more power in the phone right here in my pocket than I do in my computer sitting on my desk at home."

If computer manufacturers had conducted SWOT analyses, there was no way that they saw the rise of mobile phones coming. A mobile phone is not an obvious direct competitor in the same market space as a computer. Just like there was no way that firms producing typewriters saw the rise of computers, there was no way for computer manufacturers using SWOT analyses to foresee the rise of mobile phones.

Ohmae's 3C Model

So if SWOT analyses aren't useful in today's markets with their lower barriers to entry and rise of indirect competitors, what about other strategic planning models? Ohmae's 3C model, for instance? Corporate strategist Kenichi Ohmae, former senior partner in McKinsey and former President of UCLA, suggested that all corporate strategies really flowed from customers. On the face of things, this sounds logical. But let's dig deeper. In Ohmae's 3C model, the *customers* which a company serves, and how a firm serves those customers, defines its strategy. The relationships between the company and its competitors are all defined in relation to its customer base. To Ohmae, the primary goal of business is to serve the interests of the customer—as in, the old-fashioned type of customer who directly purchases your product right now, and not shareholders, employees, or external stakeholders such as the general public.

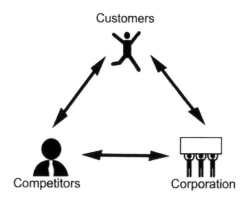

Yet, in reality, not all companies primarily serve customers, as Ohmae predicted that they should. (Again, we don't live in an idealized world where the perfect parabola or perfect business model really works. Far more useful, to my mind, is a practical model regardless of how pretty it looks). Many highly successful, leading-edge companies today aren't driven by what their *current customers* need or even want. These companies may be focused on *shareholders*—since by benefitting investors, they receive the funds that they need in order to accomplish the work that they want to do. Or they may focus on *future customers*, since high tech software companies often realize that only a small percentage of their software users are ever early adopters, and that these early adopters differ in their needs from the future users who dot the broader landscape and whom will later become the bread and butter of their business. Many firms work hard to support installed customer bases, in hopes of retaining these clients over the long term.

In the words of a large software company's employee:

> When you have an installed customer base, you have installed products in the market; you can't really stop supporting those, otherwise you risk losing those customers in the future. I get the feeling we're not quite as nimble as we wish we could be, but it's for good reasons, you know, it's not because people are stuck in saying, 'Oh, we don't want to change.' It's, 'Well, we're going to change, but we can't expect our customers to change as quickly as that and so, we still need to support them in what they've already purchased from us.'

In the words of another well-known software company's Director:

> I think that the customer is always the focus; you know when we say the customer, the customer's not the buying public, it's the people that are using our products.

A Software Engineer concurred:

> Driving right to the user to try to get the best possible experience for the user, that's the motivation.

Several companies focused closely on their shareholders. In the words of a Chief Technical Officer,

> Ultimately, we exist for our [shareholders] you know, we are a for-profit company, we exist for our shareholders to be able to have an enterprise [in which] to invest.

Porter's Generic Strategies

Harvard Business School Professor Michael Porter suggested that there were several "generic" strategies or approaches which all companies could pursue in order to gain competitive advantage. In order to differentiate itself from competitors, Porter suggested that a firm had three options:

(1) To compete on cost—lowering their prices

(2) To invest time and R&D funds to differentiate their product

(3) Narrow their market scope to better serve the needs of a particular customer segment and develop customer closeness

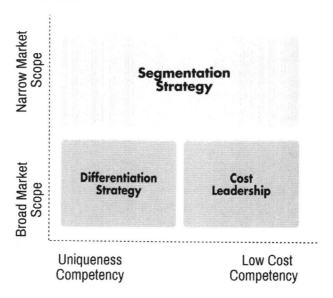

In Porter's approach, all a company has to do in order to differentiate itself from its competitors is to do a quick survey of others in the industry (whether by benchmarking datasets, Google searches, or through scrolling through a list of industry classification codes), to figure out what basis they are competing on—whether low cost or new innovation, or service of some very particular customer base—and then go and compete on some other basis. In other words, a company just has to figure out what others are doing, then figure out what they themselves have been doing—and then simply change whatever it is that they've been doing. This all seems very simple and reasonable on the surface. But in practice, it's difficult to tell who the competition really is. While government and academic publications as well as business magazines speak about industry classifications, when I spoke to those in industry, and asked what industry their firms were in, I often got blank stares or puzzled looks. In the words of a Vice President:

> It depends on the business. Across the board, in fairness, let's just say the competitor we run into most often across all of our businesses is ZZZ because they participate in our primary industry, they participate in the secondary business, and I would tell you, in those spaces we have more share almost across the board than they do with the exception of probably our tertiary business. Where we participate in the same products and services they do. So we don't play with T products, so you take that out, but in the tertiary business, its scale. They bought three companies, so they're bigger than we are. But, we compete very nicely with them head to head; now that said, they're also, what, 10, 15 times our size? And they compete in a bunch of other markets we don't compete in, so it's hard.

A PDP Lead at a manufacturing company didn't mince words:

> In our key products, we have more market share than the competition. And in our growing products, we are trying to take market share, so, not a leader there.

Business Reality

While traditional strategic tools like Porter's assume that companies are competing in general industry spaces, like many players playing against one another across a single tennis court, this model of the business world doesn't bear out. Companies don't compete head to head with their direct competitors. These competitors might have significant first-mover advantage—brand recognition, established customer relationships, smooth supply chains, and R&D pipelines. Competing head to head with a competitor on their own turf would be crazy, and increase risk exponentially.

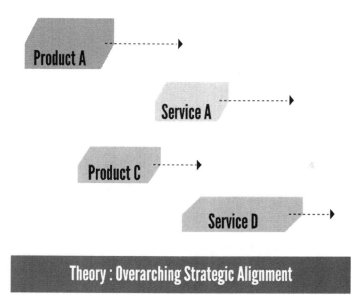

Nor do companies follow a single generic strategy. Although many companies and consultants try to describe their strategy in terms of a simple, single direction, the business reality is a whole lot more complex.

Even among smaller companies, several product lines existed, with each product following its own strategy for competing in a *niche*—a specific narrower area of focus which competitors had failed to take up. Instead of thinking of a singular overarching "strategy" with a capital "S," it is much more useful to think of several smaller strategies.

This is as true in large, global companies as small ones. "When you're trying to make a name for yourself as a seed investor, the name of the game is *differentiation*," according to Johnny Hwin, a San Francisco tech entrepreneur and investor. Differentiation by competing in narrower niches is a strategy of large, global companies as much as start-ups. Thinking about strategy in terms of generic types fails to describe strategy in the manner in which it is successfully carried out in industry.

Each product or service offering is meant to appeal to a slightly different audience. Even within your own company, you may be appealing to the premium customers seeking greater features, differentiation, and support, as well as the value customers looking for a great price rather than service down the road. You do not have to appeal to the whole range of customers with each and every product you put out to market, for to do so would be foolhardy—but being aware of the customers, the segments, the price points, the service needs, and competition for each segment is important. Instead of thinking of strategy as one big plan, it is far better to think of a plurality of strategies. In active companies in rapidly changing contexts, two parts of the company may be concurrently heading in two different directions—each to better meet the needs of their specific customer base. This not a bad thing; this is a new reality for companies facing the globalization, intensification, and decentralization of markets. It is an emerging strategy for success.

Almost every company—no matter how small—typically offers several packages of products or services to meet the varying needs of different customer bases. One very small company I worked with in the past had two product offerings plus services. I mention this because it is by no means uncommon for even small companies to offer both products *and* services—an idea that is unheard-of in the academic literature, which has long implied that companies—even very large ones—are either service providers or product companies, but never both.

Instead of thinking about fitting your strategy into a *single* particular environment, based on what has spelled success in the past, perhaps it is better to think about what *direction* the market may be heading. Opportunity always lays not in doing things the same ways as competitors, merely replicating what has been, but by doing things differently. As Einstein so eloquently put it, "Insanity is doing the same thing over and over and expecting different results."

Any given product or service varies along six dimensions:

Cost (Is an offering value priced or a premium product?)

Innovation (Does the product apply a proven technology, or is it radical/innovative?)

Customization (What is the level of customization available? Is it off-the-shelf or totally customized?)

Marketing (How is the product marketed? Is it highly visible with significant brand value, or is it positioned more generically?)

Service and Support (Are customers ready to DIY—and assemble everything themselves as with IKEA furniture, or do they expect a high level of education about the product and support in using or repairing it?)

Quality (Is the product disposable or a reliable, high quality product which will last for years?)

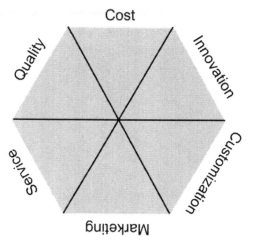

As hockey great Wayne Gretzky said, "I skate to where the puck is *going to be*, not where it *has been*." You don't succeed by moving to where the market has been, but by competing in the area where you think it is going. Only *has-beens* travel to where the market has been. It makes no sense to repeat what has succeeded in the past—because you'll likely find yourself in a saturated market, where the demand is no longer as strong. It takes a while for a business to gain traction. Markets change. Customer demand shifts. If you gear up to serve an existing successful *market niche*, chances are, something is apt to change in the intervening months, which will shake the market.

You can skate to where the puck is traveling—or where the profitable market will be—by identifying product and service dimensions. In order to skate to where the puck is likely to be, you have to understand both *where you are* located in the ice rink, and *what direction* you are skating in. In the action of the game, with the adrenaline pumping and the clock ticking, it is often difficult to think about the direction of travel. That's why it's important to walk through a strategic assessment.

In the event that a particular customer base's demand shifts, this approach protects a firm against market shocks which could lead to a company's insolvency. And since each product offered meets the needs of a different clientele, each product also faces off against a different set of competitors. Each offering is really in its own arena; therefore, it is important to conduct a strategic assessment for each and every one of the plural products or services that you are offering.

Exercise V: Defining Our Product/Service Offering

For *each* product or service offering, chart where your company's offering lies along the continuum.

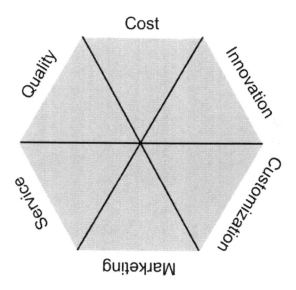

Instructions:

To complete this grid, think of each segment as its own continuum. Locate **high** values towards the outer edges of the hexagon. Locate **low values** closest toward the center of the hexagon.

1. Where does your offering currently fall along the cost continuum?

    Low   High

    ⟵——————————————————⟶

2. Where does your offering currently fall along the innovation continuum?

    Low   High

    ⟵——————————————————⟶

3. Where does your offering currently fall along the marketing continuum?
    Low   High

    ⟵——————————————————⟶

4. Where does your offering currently fall along the customization continuum?

    Low   High

    ⟵——————————————————⟶

5. Where does your offering currently fall along the service continuum?

    Low   High

    ←——————————————————————————————→

6. Where does your offering currently fall along the quality continuum?

    Low   High

    ←——————————————————————————————→

6 | Becoming:
Managing Risk

"Nature is relentless and unchangeable, and it is indifferent as to whether its hidden reasons and actions are understandable to man(kind) or not." – Galileo Galilei

In the days before Galileo, the moon was thought to be a translucent and perfect sphere, an "eternal pearl to magnificently ascend into the heavenly empyrean," according to the writer Dante. Yet, when Galileo turned his telescope to the moon and saw strange spottedness in the waning of the crescent, because of his artistic training, he understood that the patterns of light and shadow were topological markers. He realized that the deep shadows were quarries of craters and bright spots like peaks of mountains. At once, Galileo realized that the moon was not a smooth pearl, as he had been taught. Galileo then began to create topological charts, even estimating the heights of mountains on the moon.

Before Galileo, the moon's imperfections were unseen; the moon was considered perfect and ideal. Yet, just because the imperfections hadn't been identified didn't mean that the craters and the mountains didn't exist. Business risk is a lot like the craters and mountains on the moon. When we operate under the assumption that the mountains don't exist, our risk becomes much greater. By knowing and observing reality, business risk can be reduced.

When you look at risk, you have to understand that risk can essentially be understood as potential "hidden costs." These are costs which *could occur*—perhaps with some probability that can be calculated. Any time you have risk, it's like making a bet on a more positive outcome. For example, let's say your company has a great new product which, if released now, could bring in significant revenue. But, this product has a few quirks which haven't quite been ironed out yet. As such, one in every hundred products has about a 50% chance of causing minor injury to the users. So what should you do? Would you release the product? What might change that decision? Would it matter if you knew that a competitor was working on a similar release, and you were in a rush to market? Or would it still be better to "play it safe"?

Companies rightly try to reduce potential hidden costs and downsides which can endanger their bottom line. In the airline industry, there is a lot of expense that can go into maintaining aging aircraft—reinforcing the wings, reducing rust, tuning engines. Now, an airline could replace an older airplane with a brand new one, depending on its condition, but that could cost even more than just repairing the old plane. The risk is if an airplane isn't properly maintained, it could crash. This is obviously bad for the customers, the pilots, and even publicity. But, sometimes the cost of airplane maintenance dramatically outpaces the potential costs of reimbursing the families of passengers killed in a crash— making the small increase in risk a great temptation. What's the right thing to do? Given the situation, many airlines in fact delay costly routine maintenance in service of the bottom line.

There are many ways to model the trade-offs between risk and reward.

The challenge is that although there are many potential ways of mathematically calculating risk, including decision matrices and Pugh charts, to help decide what constitutes an "acceptable" level of risk—which often varies by company and product—many risks remain under the radar, and may not be recognized at all until it's too late. For example, on an individual level, it may be viewed as "less costly" to consume a typical U.S. diet of highly processed foods, meats, sugars, and refined grains. Not only does the U.S. diet cost about $550 less per person per year than a diet meeting health officials' nutrition guidelines, but processed foods take less time to prepare, may be highly portable when you're on the run, and last longer in your refrigerator because of all the preservatives. All of these are almost immediate benefits. Yet, over the long term, such a diet can be linked to chronic diseases like obesity, diabetes, and heart disease and as such has the potential to significantly increase health care costs. These costs may be far greater economically than the direct savings attributed to the diet. But I suspect we all know someone who chooses the fast food diet anyway—maybe because they're a "too busy" to bother, or like the immediate convenience of eating pre-packaged food.

Similarly, at the organizational level, companies may be driven by immediate and short-term successes, such as profitability or strategies which center on direct competitors while ignoring the rising indirect competition. For example, in the mid-2000's, several computer manufacturers focused on making their laptops lighter, thinner, and more portable—yet failed to see that smart phones were adding many of the capabilities that their devices offered—but at a much lower cost.

The problem is that the risks and expenses that we do see tend to be direct and shorter-term. Yet, in many decisions, we tend to neglect the indirect, longer-term, and tangential impacts which can have far larger repercussions for ourselves and our companies in the future. Like near-sighted individuals (myself included!) who clearly see the fine print close-up, companies can easily see to the next quarter. It is far more difficult for myopic companies to see three, five, or fifteen years down the road. Companies can squint and focus until they get headaches, but their long-term strategy is fuzzy and unclear. Often, being near-sighted, companies can't see the risk until they nearly crash into it—like an unanticipated obstacle in the road—and in their rush to course correct, often end up swerving into a ditch. This reason is that what we see as a visible and immediate risk is not the only risk. Moreover, meeting the needs of a short-term risk often has a cost—which happens to be a trade-off for longer-term risks.

For example, a lot of larger companies today tend to see the extreme costs and uncertain payoffs to funding internal innovation. As a result, they hesitate to engage in high risk internal research and development and may focus on applied technologies. Each innovation constitutes a huge risk not only for regulated companies in areas such as medical device, food and drug, and airlines and airline manufacturers, but also unregulated companies with large and diverse customer bases often feel constrained to pursue more generic designs in order to prevent alienating customer segments in their broad consumer base. If a product looks too "edgy," it may appeal to only a tiny fraction of the broader customer base. As a result, the company's product designs may look more muted and subdued to retain the broad appeal.

For example, car manufacturers since the 1950s and '60s have done away with "tail fins," "suicide doors," and more radical designs which tend to have only a limited appeal. They have generally gone away from vibrant paint colors to stick to more sedate red, white, blue, gray, and black color schemes (with sometimes a green, gold, or brown thrown in for good measure).

Similarly, if you go to the hardware store, products from drills to kitchen sinks to dishwashers are likely to look substantially similar no matter the brand, because they are designed for mass-appeal.

Producing a successful product is always inherently risky, and must meet a number of key criteria. In order for a product to succeed in market, it is not enough to merely be good. It must get several things *simultaneously* right. In a sense, all of the stars must align for something great to happen.

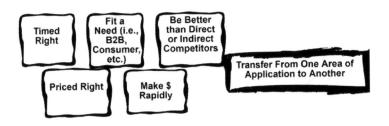

First and foremost, a product must **fit a need**. In economically uncertain times, such an offering shouldn't be just a vitamin—a "nice to have" product, but an aspirin—a "need to have," something that solves people's headaches and compels them to buy now. In economic downturns, products need to be more attractive nice interfaces, packaging, or color schemes. They must *do something*—preferably something useful, which is already being done by consumers, but at a personal cost of time and significant effort, or at a greater economic cost than the product which will replace the current activity. This is why potato peelers and other useful kitchen gadgets sold well as they were being invented during the Great Depression of the 1930s. Even though many people had little cash at the time, especially for discretionary expenditures, they could see the value of saving time and reducing food scrap. And since many households were now less likely to employ staff, the time that they were saving was their own.

Likewise, sewing was once a common activity and most people's clothes were often homemade. At some point, with the advent of automation, highly efficient factories, and lower labor costs, it became more affordable to purchase a new shirt or dress than the direct costs of buying a pattern, fabric, thread, and trim and tackling the task yourself—and, if your sewing skills are anything like mine, the final product looks better, too.

Second, the product must **be somehow better** than other offerings on the market. Everyone knows that it can be deadly for a company to compete on bottom-line cost. It's like my grandpa used to tell me, "There's always going to be somebody smarter than you, there's always going to be somebody richer than you, and there's always going to be somebody better looking than you." Arguably, that same life lesson applies doubly to companies.

There will always be companies that are *smarter* than your own. Once a product has already been created, it becomes relatively simple to reverse-engineer it and for competitors to learn from your earlier mistakes. It is as Galileo himself said, "All truths are easy to understand once they are discovered; the point is to discover them." The fact that a new market entrant can copy an innovation minus its "bugs" makes a company seem "smarter" on the surface of things. But if you, as an incumbent, can take the mistakes that you made in product development and learn from them yourself, your company will be in a much better position to develop new and improved products than a firm which merely copied your products. This is because the activity builds *absorptive capacity*.

Just as lifting weights builds your individual strength and, over time, increases the amount of weight that you can bench press, the amount of heavy lifting that a company does in the process of inventing increases its capacity to do *even more* heavy lifting in the future. This is a transferable skill—since the weight you have lifted with one set of dumbbells builds the strength and internal capacity to lift other weights as well (be they another set of dumbbells, heavy boxes, hot baking pans, or other weights you need to lift as you go about your daily living).

There will always be companies that have *deeper pockets* to spend on their product development. It's easy for them to replicate your offering, or even improve on it—rapidly—if they choose to do so. But if you find your niche, and identify some customer base which you can serve *better* than the competitors, and adapt your product to their specific purpose, you can build a strong customer loyalty. This bond makes it difficult for a richer competitor to woo your customers. Large advertising budgets can't match the saleability of a product which has some underlying quality which generates real value or savings for a customer.

There will also inevitably be companies that are *better looking* than yours. Whether they have better design, more attractive packaging, or more skilful marketing campaigns that garner broad attention, there will always be companies that are simply *beautiful*. They may be masters of the media, attract attention for engaging in superficial levels of community involvement, donate token amounts to charities, or developing skin-deep "environmentally friendly" policies. These companies may hire vast armies of customer service representatives to scour the internet and interact with customers on social media to maintain an image. These companies may cultivate an image of "cool" by allowing dogs in their office, catering in weekly restaurant lunches, providing gym memberships to their employees, or providing other perks that are viewed as being much cooler than your basic 401k plan. And these firms may truly look *beautiful* to all outward public appearance. You might find yourself asking, "How can I compete with *that*?" But you know what? It's ok. Not everyone is looking for the most beautiful product or the coolest presentation. Some customers prioritize other features or aspects over *looks*. If you're not competing on looks, those are your people. It's your job to focus on what's better than *beauty* to these customers and deliver it.

If your product has become commoditized, it's relatively easy for a competitor to come up with some clever supply chain trick to make their sourcing cheaper, or to use their firm's deep pockets to subsidize a temporary loss—just until you go bankrupt. Almost all of the management studies warn of running into the situation of commoditization. And the good news is, these are relatively easy things to do. The trick is to make your product *different*—and for your customer base, *better*. It doesn't really have to appeal to everyone—after all, an overly broad product design is what leads to commoditization in the first place.

Whatever you do, you don't want to compete head-to-head. Instead, you need to differentiate. Maybe your product is the absolute best for some specialized application or some niche customer, and you can build up their loyalty. Perhaps you can reinvest a significant portion of your profits into research and development to keep up a rapid pace of innovation that competitors can't match. Or perhaps you can focus on product quality, or customer support, or educating customers in the value and use of your product. But whatever you do, your customer needs to view your product as being different and better than not only direct competitors, but product substitutes—products that they could buy which aren't exactly your product but which might suit their purpose, more or less.

Beyond merely being somehow *better* than competitors, the offering must be **priced right**. It doesn't matter how much better your product is for a particular customer base if they just can't afford to buy it. Even if it's a premium product with premium features, it has to be affordable to some demographic.

This is no different than in many areas of business. Price plays an important role in day to day decisions. In the words of a safety manager:

> If I could sell you the safest car and you'd never get in an accident,[and] you'd never get hurt, would you buy it? And you're like "sure, OK." It's $500 million. You'd be like, "well, no." That's the same thing with safety out here. You could make everything in this building completely 100% safe but nobody would have a job, and you wouldn't produce enough parts to make it worthwhile. So you have that balance out there.

Whether you're selling an internal service like safety to your company, or an external product on the market, you have to show your customers its value—not just abstract value, but make the case in dollars and cents. And while a new product doesn't have to be "affordable" to the masses, it does have to show tangible value for the customer which is greater than the value produced by the alternatives (including the alternative of not purchasing any product).

In addition, the product must also be **timed right**. When YouTube came out, the time was ripe for the video sharing service. Any earlier, and the broadband internet made loading videos extremely slow. Any later, and chances are, a competitor would have already filled the need. Getting the timing right is probably the trickiest part of any innovation—simply because it requires the most luck. Identifying the social trends, and what people currently view as needs, while recognizing the possibilities that can be realized using today's technology requires a balancing act. If a product is too obvious, chances are that competing firms with deep pockets will take over development as soon as you have proven that there is a market. But if the need isn't completely clear to consumers, you're going to have a hard time selling it—explaining its use and benefits to customers and why there is a "need" at all.

Truly ground swelling innovations—of the type you see splashed across the Wall Street Journal's Initial Public Offering (IPO) page—meet all five of these factors to some degree. The best innovations not only fill all five needs, but frequently present the opportunity for further incremental innovation, opening up the possibility of applying this particular innovation to new contexts in the future. For example, a new spark plug developed in the automotive industry may be fruitfully applied to lawnmowers, snowmobiles, and a range of similar products. These proven innovations pose far less risk than the initial innovation—since they have proven themselves out in the market, demonstrated a customer demand, and undergone further testing and development, making it likely that early product issues have been ironed out. Yet, despite much lower risks, these proven innovations may offer just as much potential financial upside for a company, as the proven innovation is applied in a new way, creating a new market opportunity.

Because of all the potential pitfalls related to engaging in radical innovation, many large, Fortune 500 companies would rather trade cash for already-successful start-up companies, rather than do the dirty work of innovation themselves.

Several Fortune 500's have so-called "boiler rooms" filled with phone banks staffed with recent college graduates calling potential acquisitions non-stop to gauge interest and availability. By developing a dialogue, or even a courtship, with companies located in this pool of innovative firms, many large companies are able to keep their innovation pipeline filled with external sources of innovation. In a short-term view, this is a good thing for companies—trading risk, which is expensive, for cash, which is cheap. But if the journey towards innovation is worth anything—and if a company earns valuable knowledge both of what to do and what not to do by engaging in the search—simply purchasing innovation does companies a disservice. Indeed, some may liken the practice to college students buying the answer sheet to a final exam—it saves time and provides a quick short cut—but fails to provide the deeper benefits related to actually learning over the long term. Companies that completely do away with internal innovation in favour of external sourcing may dramatically increase their hidden risk, while simultaneously seeming to reduce the obvious risks of innovating.

Frequently, failure is not forever. Companies can learn just as much from their failures as they do from their product successes. By engaging in the process of innovation, companies can become attuned to potential market opportunities, generate insights about process improvements, and build the resources needed to support future development. These companies can increase their "absorptive capacity," and accelerate their potential for learning. Just like muscles are built up through lifting heavy weights, so too are the muscles of innovation. Processes which seem as if they reduce risk may have deep costs and consequences in the long-term. It is important not to be myopic when thinking about risk.

Traditional risk analyses are helpless in the face of changing market conditions where avoiding "risks" may provide a temporary advantage, at a long term cost. Like borrowing money from a bank now results in an immediate benefit, at a long-term cost, managing short term risk often incurs a long-term cost. Just as there is no such thing as a "free lunch," there is no such thing as avoiding a risk for free. There is always some cost or trade off related to every benefit.

Exercise VI: Analyzing Risk Trade-Off

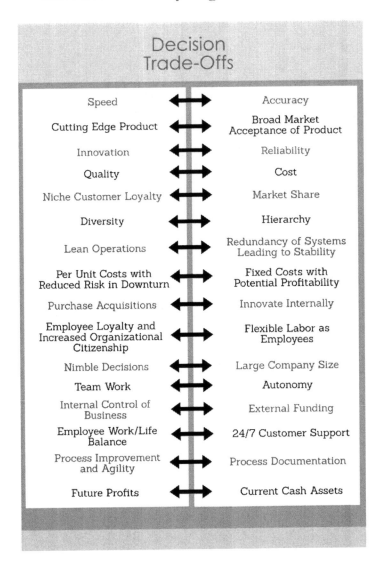

Decision Trade-Offs

Speed	Accuracy
Cutting Edge Product	Broad Market Acceptance of Product
Innovation	Reliability
Quality	Cost
Niche Customer Loyalty	Market Share
Diversity	Hierarchy
Lean Operations	Redundancy of Systems Leading to Stability
Per Unit Costs with Reduced Risk in Downturn	Fixed Costs with Potential Profitability
Purchase Acquisitions	Innovate Internally
Employee Loyalty and Increased Organizational Citizenship	Flexible Labor as Employees
Nimble Decisions	Large Company Size
Team Work	Autonomy
Internal Control of Business	External Funding
Employee Work/Life Balance	24/7 Customer Support
Process Improvement and Agility	Process Documentation
Future Profits	Current Cash Assets

1) Which risks do you currently manage? **(list out)**

2) What are the potential risks or trade-offs that result from managing that risk?

3) Are these acceptable risks? What is the alternative?

7 | Becoming: Decisioning for Results

"Don't tell people how to do things, tell them what to do, and let them surprise you with their results."
-General George Patton

Galileo was great because he was often willing to change his views based on new observations and evidence. If the data didn't match his previous assumptions, Galileo changed his mind. How many people do you know who, in the face of new evidence that their assumptions may be wrong, simply double down in their belief?

Galileo's approach was therefore somewhat unique. Today, we call his approach the *scientific method*. While Galileo's approach was generally limited to a single decision maker, reflecting the conditions of his time, in today's companies, decisioning is much more complex. Work is rarely completed by one person alone—but many people working together to create more complex products. Nevertheless, this data-driven framework can be applied to organizational decisioning to make a fresh approach. This approach can help companies to overcome myopia and errors in thinking, and reduce mistakes.

In 1963, famed management scholars Cyert and March (1963) asked a pair of key questions regarding organizational learning:

- What is the relation between decisions made by the responsible representatives and the final "decision" implemented by the organization?

And:

- In what systematic ways are decisions elaborated and changed by the organization? (Cyert & March, 1963, p. 21-22).

These are key questions which are fundamental to understanding how organizational decisioning works. Over 50 years later, these questions still have not found firm or adequate answers in the documented research. Perhaps it is because nobody has been asking the people in industry. Sure, they'll send out a survey—but rarely with the option "does not apply." This means that the data is gathered simply to *prove* a hypothesized imaginary model, rather than to *build* the model ground up from real-world data. This difference may appear semantic, but the difference is enormous.

While most of the management literature out there implies that there are three decision *types*—or distinct ways in which decisions are made, namely:

(1) top-down marching orders,

(2) bottom-up ideas driven by group consensus, or

(3) process decision-making where leadership plans the *what*, leaving the *where* and *how* to those on the frontlines.

Further, the literature suggests that each time an organization goes to make a decision that they will use this same basic decisioning approach. So, deciding whether a $50 million acquisition is a good idea? Use the decisioning approach. Deciding whether to buy a $5 monthly subscription to a piece of software? Use the same decisioning approach.

Decisioning

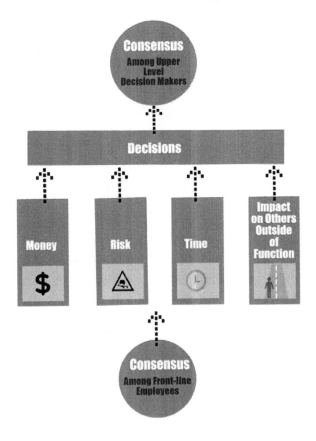

This, of course, is ridiculous. If a company were to use the same process for selecting a cheap one-off supply purchase as it used for developing a market strategy, the company would end up wasting a lot of time (and hence money) on sourcing small products, while simultaneously failing to investigate the broader implications of truly big decisions like new product strategies or big investments.

Unfortunately, as you probably already realize, the reality of decision making in today's learning organizations is a little more complicated than the notion of *decision types* allows. In complex market environments filled with rapid changes, *all* of the organizations used *all* of the decision types at one time or another. In short, what I found was that there are no hard and fast categories—decision strategies aren't really types at all.

What exist instead are categories of decisions, for which a far more fluid decisioning process is followed. The categories seem to exist mainly because who has ultimate authority for making a decision often differs depending on the context, and the different groups who need to be involved in deciding.

In the words of Marketing Manager:

> Well, I think that there are probably different levels of decisions. I suppose *strategic level* decisions that are made that are called "strategies," and then on the opportunistic side, they actively seek out the things that they can do to be competitively differentiated, so that's one level. Then another level is the *account decisions*, the kind of things that the guys who own the account manage when they collaborate. Then the third decision level is thinking about, "What are the *managerial, internal human resource* aspects? What are the key investments in people and process that can be made?" so I think that there are those three levels of decisions.

What was stunning to me was that employees didn't describe rigid types of decision making processes, as the management literature described. Instead, employees were often empowered to make decisions based on their own professional judgment, while other times, rightly left decisions to leadership. For some decisions, there were clearly top-down marching orders, while others were bottom-up ideas driven by group consensus. Yet, somehow employees knew *exactly* when to make a decision, and when to leave it up to the group and when to take it up the ladder.

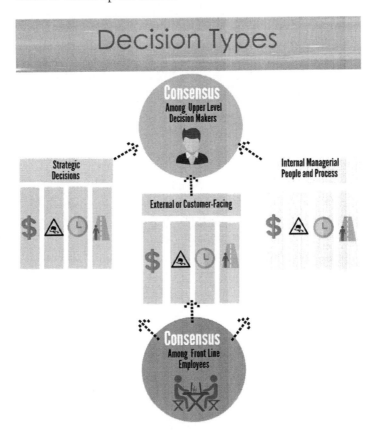

A Senior Engineering Manager described decisions as coming "typically through consensus, and if consensus can't be reached, then it'll go up the ladder."

A lot of times, employees were left to make decisions based on their own professional judgments. A Purchasing Lead at a large manufacturer put it this way:

> The company I work for is a really young organization and everybody moves really fast; you know, you're expected to perform at a very high rate and high level and not given much time to always think about what the proper answer is. We take a lot of risk because you're expected more to make an estimated guess, or use best judgment and get it done quickly versus necessarily getting it exactly right every time.

The most successful companies left a lot of things up to professionals to make a decision. But as many managers realize, it's hard to let go. Things might not necessarily turn out like you might think they "should". Things don't get done the way that you would do them. But the successful companies tend to let go of a lot—and things have turned out fine.

While we may want to control things, a lot of factors exist that are outside of our control. For example, when we are driving to work in the morning, we can control our vehicle and keep it in its lane, and we can follow the speed limit and obey the stop lights. Despite all of that control, we can't really control what's going on *around* us—if there's a hail storm, or a traffic accident up ahead, or if someone decides to suddenly swerve into our lane.

In business, leaders have may have control of how their companies manoeuver in the market—in other words, where they are steering and where they hope to get for the final destination, how they will navigate, and when to use an alternate route or keep on track. They may even control when to apply the gas to fuel a project and when to put on the breaks. Despite all this control of several variables, they can't control the economic climate, which niches competitors will try to attack (steering into your company's lane), or what emerging competitors might do. Business leaders can only steer, start, and stop.

In driving, you have to surrender some control and learn to live with uncertainty. Unfortunately, in business, many leaders would like to control everything—or feel that they are in control. I'm not sure that this is possible on a practical plane.

Despite all the uncertainty surrounding driving, insurance companies put odds on the average driver that he or she will only get into a car accident once every 10 years. It's amazing to consider when you stop to think about all of the factors that fall outside of the average drivers' control. Yet, despite all of the uncertainty, everything usually comes together, without your having full control of the situation—and you still get safely to where you're going. When you stop to think about how complex it is, you might consider it a minor miracle.

But what ensures so many safe trips is that there are a few simple, widely known, predictable rules of the road—which most people follow, most of the time. Rules like who has the "right of way," serve to prevent disagreements and crashes. Likewise, in successful companies, there exist a few simple rules which ensure that employees know exactly when to make a decision, or when to take it up the ladder.

Just as drivers across a nation follow a simple set of road rules, no matter where they are driving, employees at leading companies followed a simple, predictable set of rules for decisioning. In fact, the clearer and simpler these rules are, the more smoothly things run. "A complex system, contrary to what people believe, does not require complicated systems and regulations and intricate policies. The simpler, the better. Complications lead to multiplicative chains of unanticipated effects" (Taleb, 2012, p. 11).

The key to clear, predictable decisioning lies in four gates:

1) Money
2) Risk
3) Time or scheduling, and
4) Impact on others outside of the function

These are the pillars to effective decision-making. A Research and Development Lab Manager described the biggest challenge of his role as being one of balancing the "right" amount of information to provide employees:

> The temptation is perhaps to give everybody either nothing or to give them everything. And giving them everything becomes an overload. Giving them nothing basically doesn't allow them to see how they connect in with things. The challenge is to try and say what's the right balance here; I probably tend to balance a little bit more towards a bit more detail everybody has their own filters, and I think that a lot of people do a reasonable job of filtering down to what they need to do. I think we really work on how we simplify this down to our major priorities that we've got for the year, and then priorities for beyond that, down to our operational priorities.

In the leading companies, decision making generally moves up the hierarchy based on one or more of the four gates—in some companies, it's based on cost. Any decisions to be made at that cost or above a certain dollar amount are automatically forwarded to leadership. In other groups it may be based on cost, risk, and schedule. In some roles, it has to do with the potential for the decision to impact others outside of the function. Since those on the frontlines don't necessarily have a line of sight to know what consequences their decision will have on those in other functions, advancing the decision up a level to someone who has that perspective makes sense.

A Vice President described it this way:

> I'm not sure there's ever consensus around a plan, as much as there is support and alignment. Even within your own family, nobody agrees about where you might want go to dinner that night. But generally, people line up once somebody decides, or the majority decide. You know, we have good processes here in how plans get created. At the end of the day, though it's still a combination of senior management's vision about where we want to go and what the strategic resources are in our business, combined with the strategies that our line managers and divisional and functional leaders and their teams create.

While not all of the organizations transparently based their decision-making on all of the four gates, learning organizations would probably do well to take each of the gates into consideration to enhance the smooth running of their organizations.

To borrow another automotive metaphor, the high-performing organizations that leaders drive are a lot like sports cars. Just as sports cars have delicate engines that are susceptible to heat and cold, and must be fine-tuned in order to perform well, high performing organizations must keep their engines running smoothly. Decision-making is a key driver of organizational performance. Leaders must fine-tune their driving behaviors in order to safely operate their organizations to arrive at their final destination.

In order to fine-tune decision-making, you don't want to make the process too tight, or too loose. Frankly, there are risks in both.

Tight vs. Loose Decision Risks

Too Tightly Managed	Too Loosely Managed
Risks:	**Risks:**
Delayed Decisions, Slower Speed	Potential Unintended Consequences, Collateral Damage Across Functions
Reduced Market Responsiveness	Unnecessary Pressure on Employees Contributing to Increased Cognitive Load, Decreased Performance
Increased Potential for Misunderstandings	Increased Risk of Error in Judgement
Increased Hazard in a competitive Market	Greater Likelihood of Scheduling Problems
Less Engaged Employees	Decisions Based on Emotion Rather than Data

Risks of running too tightly

If you regulate your company too tightly, there are many inherent risks. A primary risk is that it delays the speed of decision-making. If everyone on your team, or in your group must go to you before they make a decision, or if your team is unclear on which decisions need to pass through you, everything will move at a much slower pace—and the amount of work facing you will be enormous. This need for you to touch a number of decisions outside of the four gates also has a cost in terms of delays in projects and work for each of your direct reports, as well as the work of those whom they serve. Just as an engine with a clogged hose tends to reduce the flow of fluids, the flow of work through your organization will move much more slowly. And like a clogged hose, this will cause tension as the pressure builds up, while employees continue to try to pass more and more backlogged work through a constricted channel.

Another problem that tight regulation causes is reduced market responsiveness. Even if your company does not make decisions quickly, your competitors might, causing the market to shift even if you stand still. This is a reality that we can't change. But if employees closer to the front lines are empowered to make decisions, they can meet customer needs and respond to shifts in the market more rapidly. They also often understand technical issues in a way that they may be difficult to communicate to you, whether because the insights are embedded in tacit knowledge built up through experience or because the type of knowledge is more hands-on or visual in nature and does not find its way into words easily. Frontline employees have a lot of wisdom and experience in understanding customer needs. Every time that you as a leader become involved in situations that you don't need to be in, there is significant room for error and increased misunderstandings. Since not every scenario is communicated well through words, you might be acting on a misperception of the situation, or base your response on your past experience, which may not be suited to the current situation on the ground.

While under many circumstances, it may seem wise to trust only yourself with decisions, in the long-run, by making decisions for others that may best left to them; you are disempowering people and basically saying "I don't trust you." This is not the message you want to send to your employees—if you don't trust them, you also are basically saying that you don't value them. There are no two ways about it. My most hurtful work experience involved exactly such a situation.

I once worked for a manager who didn't like to write, so when the time came to write a report for the CEO about how the companies acquired as part of a new merger were to be trained, the manager gave it to me to write and put my name on the project. I thought nothing of it, and put together market analysis, quotes from dealer interviews, and anything else I thought would be useful, along with a phased training plan. One of the sales executives somehow got hold of an early draft and distributed a copy to everyone in a meeting— everyone, of course, except my director, who felt a little left out.

But when the time came to start thinking about delivering the revised report to the CEO, my manager took my final draft and passed it around the office for each and every employee to edit and make changes. These were employees who hadn't interviewed experts, who had no idea of the product line, or the market, or the field of training itself, and who hadn't been involved in the project until just then, in the very last minute edits. As can be expected, there were a variety of changes made—from changes to strategy (which seemed like "too much work to implement") to direct quotes from internal customers ("They can ask for anything they want, but they won't get it; it's best if the executives don't even know that they asked"), to technical terms with real meanings being deemed "fluffy" simply because someone lacked a sufficiently technical background in the field. Several passages of relevant data were deleted to fit a perceived "perfect page count" since my manger did not know how to alter margins or font size in Microsoft Word. What was left at the end was, quite predictably, a mess. And although the very essence of my report was altered, I didn't get the final edit. This embarrassing work was delivered to the CEO—with mine the only my name on it. To this day, I still feel badly for the CEO, who was presented the challenge of trying to make sense of the jumble that remained.

To anyone with a sense of professionalism, and a strong professional identity, being told that you are not really trusted is a significant blow to your self-image. It is also dehumanizing in a sense, since an individual person, who has feelings, thoughts, and motivations all their own, is turned into a tool for you to achieve your own ends. While it may seem like a "win" at the time—you get the work done, in precisely the way that you envisioned it—over the long run, it wears people down; it breeds distrust, and disengages employees from their work. How excited would you be to do the next project, knowing it might be subject to drastic group edits at the very last minute? Disempowering people is a fast track way to ensuring that people develop a distaste for their work.

Tight regulation may be good for control purposes, but it's not good for employee morale, let alone developing the kind of passion for products and work that drive the innovation which is so necessary for companies today. By only taking responsibility for decisions at the four gates, you will ensure that you aren't overwhelmed with busy work. If you're making decisions about everything, there's always a chance that some detail might slip through the crack. There's no way that any one person can manage all the decisions for any organization, no matter how large or no matter how small, over the long-term. Even if you try, employees often come to resent being ruled with an iron fist. It's not a long-term strategy for success.

Making clear that you're responsible for decisions around these four gates (or any one of these, if you're in a much larger multi-national firm), and communicating this message widely, repeatedly, and clearly ensures that you won't be perceived as omniscient and all-powerful—which at first glance seems great, but in practice means that you'll be held responsible for the repercussions of all sorts of decisions that you really didn't have anything to do with. In many companies, people tend to view the leader as the cause of all functioning in the company—all the good things that happen, along with all of the bad—missed deadlines, lost customers, decreased market share, a slide in the stock price, or a lack of rain in China. Trust me when I say that it's best not to be perceived as responsible for all this!

Risks of running too loose

While small companies like GitHub and Chicago-based Software Company 37signals try a relaxed approach where employees manage themselves, or rotate management duties such as tracking group performance with a manager-of-the-month, it is possible to allow things to get too loose. In the words of 37signals designer Jason Zimdars, "We don't want to accept that we need management," he says, "but we kind of do."

If the pendulum swings too far in the opposite direction, and your organization is running too loose, you may find yourself facing a high increase in errors in judgment that suddenly all need attention at once. Once things have fallen apart, everything is usually urgent, and many of the issues may now be compounded, making them more difficult to fix. It's almost always easier to do things correctly in the first place, than to try to fix them afterward—it's like trying to un-break an egg. Nor can things always be "fixed." In the children's rhyme Humpty Dumpty, "all the king's horses and all the king's men couldn't put Humpty together again." Immense efforts and allocated resources to "fix" things can't always repair a firm once the damage is done. Allow too many errors in judgment, and things can get completely out of hand. Companies build their reputation based on the things that they do. If your company builds a reputation for making mistakes—no matter how quickly and neatly they fix them—you may lose trust.

It has been suggested that you need five positive interactions with customers, for each negative interaction, in order to retain a positive reputation. If you have more negatives than that, the company reputation is likely to be damaged.

A second consequence of running on pure empowerment for decision-making is that there is a greater likelihood of running into scheduling problems. If someone makes a decision in their own function, and it impacts people in other departments, the decision-maker may not have a line of sight to his or her peers in the other departments and what those impacts might be. He or she is basically decisioning based on tunnel vision—what's best for that immediate department alone. Some groups such as manufacturing have a lot of front-line decisions that they could be making, but these decisions might have consequences for other groups. Choosing a new part—such as a screw instead of a bolt—it may save time in installation, but the decision is also likely to affect the supply chain group, who suddenly needs to scramble to order more screws to fill the increasing demand, and training who needs to document the new process, and engineering, who really probably should test if the screw is going affix the part to the product as well as the bolt did—before shipping the product out to customers. If people on the front lines in a single department are unaware of the potential repercussions of their decision for other departments, they cannot maximize their decisions and create the most good for the most people. They aren't likely to do what's best for the organization, because they don't know all of the possible factors. A decision based on a single factor—"what's good for my group" may not be ideal for the company as a whole.

Such decisions also tend to frequently run into scheduling problems. A delay here or there may seem like "no big deal" within one group, but delays tend to compound themselves and have a ripple effect on other groups. If a deadline in development slips by a day or two, it might mean that groups downstream like customer service or training and development have to scramble to prepare for a launch date. Companies that run loose often allow multiple deadlines to slip and as a result, launch dates often pass without consequence, because it is very difficult to reign in scheduling while also empowering employees to make decisions themselves—even though each of these decisions have an impact on the schedule. You may convince yourself that "there's a learning curve" in scheduling well, and "eventually everyone will get there," but it's not simply a logistic of allowing employees to control their own schedules and learn how to do that well; there are things about the company, about other groups' projects, and about competing timelines that many employees simply are not privy to knowing. Even if individuals schedule their time well, their lack of knowledge about other groups' scheduling conflicts almost certainly will impact their perfect schedule sooner or later, and they personally will end up looking like mud. The best performing companies don't put their employees in a position to fail. No amount of holding employees' feet to the fire will solve the issue of an employee-planned schedule falling apart. You can get angry, and hold your employees responsible for things that really are beyond their control, and play the blame game when things fall apart, and you can hold your breath and turn red and tantrum like a toddler, or you can get wise and realize that it simply isn't effective to empower employees to make decisions that affect scheduling. Just as you don't want to be held responsible for events that occurred *before* your tenure, or disasters that happened that are *outside your realm of authority*, employees don't want to be responsible for things *they* can't control. And employees can't control what they don't know; they may not even know what it is that they don't know—until it's too late. Unless *all* departments reveal *all* of the projects they're working on—even the "top secret" ones—and continue to keep their schedules completely updated, it's just not effective to allow employees to set scheduling decisions that will affect others. And even in the rare organization where employees do know all the pieces, it still may not be the most efficient way of doing things.

The next risk of a too loose decision-making process is clear: if you hold employees responsible for the consequences of their decisions, especially those decisions affecting the four gates—money, risk, time, and impact—they will probably be stressed out. Sure, it may feel like a vacation for you not to have to make difficult decisions, but for the employees who take up the decision-making duty, there will be increased pressure. Nobody wants to make the "wrong" decision. This pressure will increase employees' *cognitive load*. The way to think about cognitive load is to think about a camel in the desert carrying loads. Now, each employee's mind is sort of like a camel. Unloaded, it can travel quickly at a certain rate. Or, it carries a certain amount of details and pressure. But the more you load it down, the slower it goes. As you start adding stress, the employee who could travel quickly begins to work slower and slower. The work itself becomes less detailed and less creative. As you increase employee cognitive load, you decrease performance, and reduce the potential for innovation. According to Christine Porath of the University of Southern California's Marshall School of Business and Amir Erez of the Warrington College of Business Administration at the University of Florida, the mere *thought* of being on the receiving end of verbal abuse or blame hurts people's ability to perform complex tasks requiring creativity, flexibility, and memory recall.

Instead of adding pressures—especially for making decisions around the four gates—it may be wise to focus your employees on efforts that they are able to accomplish, such as technical work. It really reduces team performance and task performance to spread the management load around. In a competitive environment where companies are increasingly being asked to move quickly, distributing *all* of the decision-making around the company is really the wrong call. There needs to be a balance. As a multinational company's Learning Specialist described it:

> As in most things, I think there's power in the middle. When you're too strong one way or another, you start having problems of applicability and sustainability.

Decisions *outside* of the four gates are best left to employees, who can act fast and be trusted to do their best professionally. Decisions *within* the four gates are management's job. Control just these four managerial things, and you can control the market. Try to control more, and you're apt to lose control. Fail to control these four and chaos will ensue. Control just four, and no more.

Balanced consensus

What was most surprising to me about the decision-making approach that members of leading companies described was the balance inherent in the model. Consensus processes were conducted at both the front-lines, and then gated, and if the decision escalated, it was often decided through consensus at the top levels. This implied that a sort of reciprocity occurred. This balanced consensus—between members at one level or another meant that a range of perspectives were captured within each decision. It also implied a certain level of respect between management and front-line employees.

What the Four Gates Imply for Functional Engagement

While all of the four gates are significant at the macro level, across the entirety of a company, not all groups are impacted by each of the four gates equally. The R&D group is not necessarily going to be overwhelmed by time constraints when developing a new product for launch. But the manufacturing group, rushing to get products out the door, may find time constraints incredibly important.

Moreover, some types of functions tend to be impacted differently than others. Functions that are traditional functions—for instance, engineering or accounting—which have a strong basis of core technical knowledge to them, and have clearly defined disciplinary bounds benefit from the potential to make a greater number of technical decisions, uninhibited by their potential impact on other groups. Engineers can safely be empowered to make a design decision that meets basic performance and cost criteria. Accountants can often select from a number of good approaches to deal with cost and numbers, based on their professional expertise.

Members of cross-functional groups—that is groups which do not necessarily have a specific domain, but which serve other groups; for instance, groups like knowledge management, training and development, organizational development, and environmental health and safety—by their very nature will find more of their decisions impeded by outside groups and those groups' constraints.

Matrixed Roles

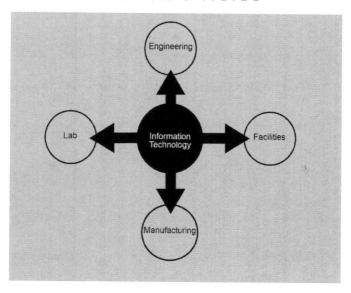

If an environmental health and safety manager wants to design a new and significant safety initiative, he or she will not only be bounded by cost, but by the schedules and even the priorities of others.

Groups that are cross functional—for example, human resources, environmental health and safety, documentation, and IT—exist to serve other groups, and are more likely than others to be tightly bounded by the four decision criteria ($, impact on others, schedule, risk) and are less likely to be able to make empowered decisions. Individuals in such functions are less likely to have the opportunity to enjoy being given free-reign over a technical project. Because of this need to "toe the line," and adjust their expectations in order to better serve others, extra measures or special means of engagement should be taken because people in these functions are less likely to have project empowerment as a primary driver of workplace engagement.

The role of a leader in the most successful organizations is rather like that of a lifeguard—to watch the group and jump in for a rescue only when the team is drowning. According to an Engineer in a company with a highly autonomous culture:

> Most of our projects do have a decision maker, so for example, in the current one that I'm in, there's a guy by name Max who is a decision maker, but that means that he will step in and make decisions only if there is a lack of consensus. If we're not converging towards consensus, then he will step in and decide one way or the other. But if otherwise, he will let the team to evaluate pros and cons. Most of the decisions are not based on subjective opinions; you have to back it up in terms of substantial data or possible solid proof, saying that "position A is better than position B so adopt solution A," so it's a very data-driven decision process. Of course there are some design decisions where you don't have any prior knowledge and you're not too sure, so that those are the cases where consensus is not easy to evolve, and if it is dragging along and impacting the deliverable of the product, the decision maker will come in and just look at everyone's ideas.

In the words of an R&D Vice President:

> My managers, my directors, my engineers, my technicians, my scientists have an awful lot of bandwidth to be able to do what they need to do when they need to do it and they're empowered until they prove to me that they can't do it.

To a Parts Manager the question of who made the final decisions came down to simple economics, "Unless it's big dollars, I'd say its consensus."

Keeping decisions relatively loose was considered a major recipe for success by a product engineer, "To me, constraints are the enemy of innovation." By keeping decision constraints to an absolute minimum, his workforce was able to imagine a greater range of possibilities—leading to greater innovation.

Exercise VII: Coordinating Decisioning

Tools:

1. What $ amount, or $ amount over budget should people come to you for?

    ┌──┐
    │   │
    │   │
    │   │
    └──┘

2. What types of risk should your reports talk to you about?

    ┌──┐
    │   │
    │   │
    │   │
    └──┘

3. What time should your reports come to you? (At risk of being over schedule? at a certain amount of time overschedule? for a project that will take up a certain amount or percent of job time?)

    ┌──┐
    │   │
    │   │
    │   │
    └──┘

4. What impact on others outside of your function should your reports see you about? (Is it outside of project scope? does it involve changes outside of particular product?)

    ┌──┐
    │   │
    │   │
    │   │
    └──┘

Decisioning

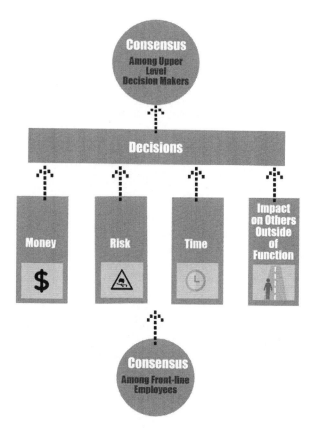

8 | Becoming: Managing Knowledge

"The increase of known truths stimulates the investigation, establishment, and growth of the arts." — Galileo Galilei

Galileo recorded his observations of the moon night after night. By his careful recording of notes in lab notebooks, he was able to see patterns coalesce from the data, and by seeing those patterns take shape, many innovations were made possible. If Galileo had not recorded his observations, would he have seen the patterns? How much innovation would have occurred? Recording and managing knowledge is instrumental in making future innovation possible. Inventions are generative, and tend to facilitate future invention.

The recognition of patterns in mountains of evidence has helped scientists to discover regularities, develop theories, and classify information. The ability to recognize patterns helps to transform piles of mere data into actionable information. If *seeing is believing*, then identifying patterns constitutes wisdom. As a traditional Indian story tells it, the goddess Sarasvati is the personification of wisdom. Sarasvati rides a swan, which is able to separate the pure cream from the mixture of water and cream which it drinks in. Wisdom, then, lies in being able to discern what is valuable from the vast ocean of information in which we now swim.

By having the data in hand, we are able to recognize repeated patterns which otherwise would not have been visible. As a result, better informed decisions can be made. We reduce our chances of making the same mistakes over and over, and can improve our performance. There is nothing more practical than basing decisions on data. This information—when arranged in a way which facilitates its everyday use and the recognition of patterns—becomes organizational knowledge.

This organizational knowledge has a real, tangible value. Peter Drucker called this era the "knowledge economy" (Drucker, 1999). Current estimates suggest that 2/3 of a company's value is based on intellectual capital and intangibles. This is far more value attributed to ideas than in the past. Yet, a company's knowledge serves as a key driver of innovation, provides fuel for new product development, and generates tangible, short-term profit.

As the barriers to entry for new companies continue to fall, driven by the trends of globalization, deregulation, and the rise of internet commerce, ever greater numbers of new companies are likely to start up and enter the market. At the same time, company knowledge is likely to increase in value, given its role in securing a company's competitive advantage. Unless a company exists in a monopoly with high or impossible barriers to entry, incumbents can no longer look to the high initial costs of starting up to protect them from the waves of new entrants. In the knowledge economy, products and services which remain plain vanilla, and fail to continually develop and evolve are likely to become commoditized much more quickly than in the past. As products become viewed as commodities, low price becomes the only value proposition that a company can offer to customers. No company can survive for long competing only on the basis of low price. Chances are, somebody new will come along with lower infrastructure and development costs who can sell the same products or services (or acceptable product substitute) for less than you do.

Learning Organization: Academic Definition

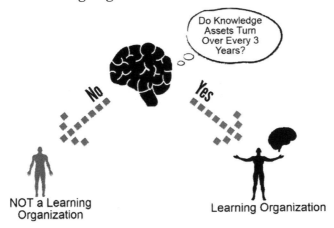

Beyond mere tangible value, the value of managing knowledge is immeasurable—in part because it is hard to guess where the next applied invention is likely to come from. Having many data points to base decisions on is useful. Despite a widespread belief that *learning organizations* can be distinguished from organizations more generally, by seeing if a firm turns over its *entire* knowledge base every three years, I have found no evidence that this is the case. While this wild belief is encapsulated in many current surveys, including the large-scale OECD innovation survey among others, and national policies are based on this very assumption, asking people at leading high performing companies the question in an open ended way revealed that the question itself didn't make a lot of sense. It is a bit outrageous to assume that learning organizations consist *solely* of those companies which turn over all of their product knowledge, all of their design knowledge, and all of their expertise every three years. This was not true even of the fast-paced software companies, where product development can often occur at a quicker pace than in many other industries due to regulation, infrastructure, and retooling demands.

Instead, asking the question, "Would you say that your organization has had more new knowledge entering the organization over the past 3 years, or would you say it has been building up over a longer period of time?" is a lot like asking the question, "Which came first, the chicken or the egg?" Companies build on underlying capabilities, which enable them to see new things, allowing them to apply these ideas in new ways, leading them to innovate. The underlying relationship between long-term knowledge held and recent innovation is inextricable.

To a manufacturing company's Marketing Manager:

> I would say it's interesting, because as I try and think about the improvements that we've had over time, it's not a continuum. There are some changes that happen; we try something and it works, and so we continue to refine that.

Products build on products, which enable other, new products to be built. Given that knowledge builds on knowledge and makes possible other potential innovations that would be unimaginable without the underlying knowledge base, it is not enough simply to create knowledge. Within a firm, knowledge must be shared and managed in order to generate value and fulfil its full potential.

Some companies invest huge amounts in research and development (R&D), but don't see much value in training and development (T&D), which they write off as an "expense." Even more companies see so little value in having expertise in formal adult training methodologies that they hire subject matter experts (SMEs) with backgrounds as various as nursing, manufacturing, elementary education, or family and home economics to create the training. I doubt that many of these companies would do the same when staffing roles they view as "mission critical."

Yet, Research and Development and Training and Development are two parts of a larger continuum—generating and dispersing knowledge. R&D can't realize its full value if the innovation isn't communicated and understood. Innovations can't be applied if they aren't known. If you innovate without communicating, in practical terms, it's the same as if you haven't innovated at all. Both require a specific knowledge and expertise, and both have a role to play in ensuring a strong and steady innovation pipeline with clear knowledge flows.

But between the two ends of the knowledge spectrum—somewhere between developing knowledge and ensuring its distribution—lies a role for everyone. If people's unique skills aren't being harnessed for the purpose of organizational learning, or if only a few people are taken to task when job-necessary knowledge isn't distributed to those who need to know, then a company isn't likely to succeed.

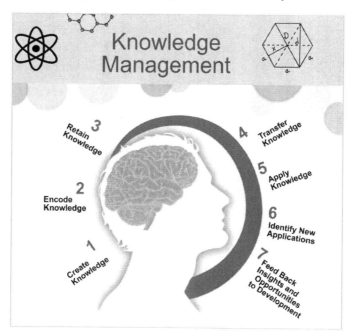

1. **Create Knowledge.**

    What: New product development. Comes up with new ideas or possible opportunities.

    Who: (i.e., R&D)

    Role: (i.e., R&D ideates early in the development process or screens product ideas from outside groups based on internally developed criteria)

2. **Encode Knowledge.**

    What: Writes down or otherwise documents knowledge. Documentation can include process knowledge, lab notebooks, or other materials.

    Who: (i.e., Knowledge Management, Process Development, Documentation)

Role: (i.e., the Documentation group reviews documents with special attention to whether a given document meets company standards for formatting, level of specification, use of a given terminology, compatibility with other documents and systems)

3. **Retain Knowledge.**

   What: Ensures that past lessons learned remain accessible, whether this information was formally documented or is preserved in informal lessons—such as stories, tribal knowledge, hands-on demonstrations, work-based learning, company "ways of doing things," or other means.

   Who: (i.e., Manufacturing "old timers," Document Repository Specialists, Learning and Development)

   Role: (i.e., Manufacturing "old timers" train new employees in manufacturing "best practices" through hands-on demonstrations upon their hire)

4. **Transfer Knowledge.**

   What: Interfaces with multiple groups to ensure that knowledge and information is shared between them.

   Who: (i.e., Training and Development, Documentation, Environmental Health and Safety)

   Role: (i.e., Training and Development provides Sales teams with information and specifications relating to their new products, passing on information from the R&D group)

5. **Apply Knowledge.**

> **What:** Takes abstract or general company knowledge (i.e., a new company policy, a new procedure, or data) and applies it to specific situations related to their role.
>
> **Who:** (i.e., Sales and Marketing, Applications, Manufacturing, Customer Service, Design)
>
> **Role:** (i.e., Customer Service reads the bulletin from Design Engineering about a weakness in an engine component. Customer Service then determines what this component's failure might look in actual equipment operation so that they can identify the issue as it occurs in the field and prepares their script for responding to customers)

6. **Identify New Applications.**

> **What:** Knowing the inventions that the company has in the pipeline, and connecting the inventions that currently exist with potential opportunities to use them.
>
> **Who:** (i.e., everyone)
>
> **Role:** (i.e., Sales, after hearing a customer's needs, recognizes a new opportunity to apply a technology)

7. **Feedback Insights and Opportunities to Research and Development.**

> **What:** Communicating insights from on-the-job learning and potential opportunities back to early stage product development teams to review feasibility.
>
> **Who:** (i.e., Sales, Training, Manufacturing)
>
> **Role:** (i.e., after recognizing a potential opportunity, communicating this opportunity to the early phase Developers for review)

New knowledge and innovation doesn't always come from R&D, but can come from the front lines as well. In the words of a manufacturing engineer:

> We are always looking for something new. We go to trade shows, and look at the new equipment, and new processes, and try to see how to apply it to our product. We got into laser-cutting a number of years ago when it was an emerging technology. It actually has allowed us to change the way we design our product. And in order to get that message across, we actually had to bring the designers from headquarters down here and show them the new capabilities of this equipment, because it changed the way that they can design their parts. You know, you're no longer taking a piece of tubing and cutting it off in a saw and then milling and drilling and bending. Now you can do all that in one machine.

Companies which are able to make healthy positive connections between their departments are far more likely to build knowledge and innovations than companies which can't. As a Chief Technical Officer put it succinctly – "the goal is to make connections". Just like your brain is only as good as your synapses for connecting different parts together, your organization's success depends on making healthy connections among its parts.

A good lesson is that not everything has to be "brand new" to be successful. Many truly wonderful inventions have been innovations that are simply applied in new ways. The classic example of this is the printing press. Gutenberg watched a winepress at work, and came up with the idea of pressing out typeface for books by using the same mechanism. This resulted in many dramatic and radical changes in society—ranging from increased literacy to the rise of authorship as a viable career. Yet, despite its dramatic impact, the printing press was not a wholly new concept—it was merely an application of the already-proven *press* to the task of printing words.

Thomas Edison held 1,039 U.S. Patents, and was no doubt an innovative individual. Yet, his invention of the electric pen—a pen that contained a small needle that moved in and out, and poked holes in paper to create a stencil—was in many ways an application of an earlier invention used by artists. In Renaissance Italy, artists painting frescoes commonly sketched their work on paper before starting on the frescoes. Once they had selected good large-scale sketches to work from, they poked holes in the paper, and affixed the sketches to the wall. The artists patted the drawings with bags of charcoal, which made dotted lines of the figures on the wall—providing a *copy* of their sketch. Apprentices often outlined these charcoal dotted lines in ink to prepare for the fresco painting.

Edison borrowed the technique of making copies, and applied it to writing rather than art, spreading ink rather than charcoal directly over the stencil to make copies. Edison's pen was used by Lewis Carroll, the author of *Alice's Adventures in Wonderland*, and became a forerunner of both the Xerox machine, and today's tattoo machine. Yet, for all of its impact, Edison's electric pen was fundamentally an application of a long-proven process to a new task.

In a more contemporary example, one inventor decided to put the little blue dot generally used on chicken packaging to let consumers know if their meat has been thawed onto vials of vaccines which need to remain cold in order to stay effective. In the context of developing countries, where electricity for refrigeration isn't always as reliable as medical professionals might wish, this simple and relatively cheap solution has potentially saved millions of lives.

Many insights can come from anywhere. Making sure that these insights are captured and communicated—and just as importantly screened for relevance—can help turn an ordinary organization into a high performing organization. Companies that use only a few of their people are like car engines running on just one or two pistons—rather than the four, six, or eight, at their disposal. It is no surprise that such companies don't process key information as quickly, seamlessly, or well—and often run out of gas.

Yet, just as cars require refined fuel to power their engines—in order to prevent knocking—so do companies. In companies, this refined fuel is screened ideas—vetted before being injected into the learning process, and circulating throughout the entire organization with unpredictable consequences. Not all ideas can be cleanly applied in all contexts, and un-vetted ideas can clog up a group's work flow.

For an example, we need to look no further than Cisco Systems. An early innovator in crowdsourcing, Cisco Systems announced an external innovation competition to find an idea that would generate a new billion-dollar business (enticing participants with a $250,000 prize). This sounded like a great idea that would produce nothing but upsides—vast numbers of untapped ideas produced on the cheap, without increasing headcount or benefits costs—what could go wrong? It turns out, by externally sourcing ideas, Cisco incurred *larger costs* of reviewing solutions than if the innovation had come from *inside* of the firm, a *slower review process* due to the larger number of submissions, and *increased bottlenecks*. The firm also took on *greater legal risk*, since any of the 2,500 participants could potentially claim that Cisco stole their ideas, even if these ideas were something that Cisco was already working on. In addition, there was some risk that participants might submit ideas that belonged to others, which they held no rights over. The result of their increased investment? 2,500 participants from 104 countries submitted just 1,200 distinct ideas. That's less than one idea for every two people!

The trouble with crowdsourcing is that not all ideas are created equal. Some ideas need a lot more refinement to work—remember the "Back to the Future" flying skateboards we were promised in the 1980s? I'm still waiting... Other some ideas are just better off being abandoned. According to Washington University psychologist Keith Sawyer: "Decades of research have consistently shown that brainstorming groups think of *far fewer* ideas than the same number of people who work alone and later pool their ideas."

Determining which ideas will fuel the company, and which ideas are likely to cause engine knocking or clogged workflow depends upon knowledge of current technical capabilities, internal company culture and processes, insights from core customers, and industry knowledge.

Exercise VIII: Rating Our Octane

Low Octane   High Octane

1. How refined (or what octane) does your idea fuel need to be?

2. What are your company's current capabilities?

3. How will the ideas be communicated across the organization?

4. How long will an idea remain in the repository before being reviewed, revised, or rejected?

9 | Becoming: Seeking Riches in Niches

> "In questions of science, the authority of a thousand is not worth the humble reasoning of a single individual."- Galileo Galilei

Just as Galileo discovered that imagined theoretical models can impede real-world progress, much in business today relies on theoretical models which do not hold up to scrutiny. Today, business runs on benchmarking, and benchmarking runs on standard industry classification codes in order to compare the performance of companies. This data is used variously to create labor policies, project market size, make investment decisions, and benchmark competitors in order to adopt "industry best practices." Such data is also often used to develop job descriptions, set pay scales, and project future labor shortages. Yet, it may be that we are building all of these castles on a foundation of quicksand.

When I asked executives in leading companies what *industry* their company was in, I expected answers like "software" or "manufacturing." Instead, their answers were startling. They spoke not of competing in *industries*, but in *spaces* or *niches* or *segments*.

In the words of a manufacturing firm's Vice President:

> Well, we compete in so many different categories. Probably the competitor that we face most often is X and I would say in some spaces, we're definitely ahead of them, but there are other spaces where they beat us.

In the words of a Director:

> We typically compete with companies that are much larger than us. Company B is 40 times our size, and Companies C, D, E, and F; all those companies that I just mentioned are larger than us. And there's some that are on par with us, but most are larger than us, and then the share really differs. In the Product 1 segment, we're the leaders. In the Product 2 segment, we're neck in neck with Company B. And then we're obviously a much, much smaller share than Company D who we compete with, so it's kind of a mix.

Industry-

> 1. the aggregate of manufacturing or technically productive enterprises in a particular field, often named after its principal product: i.e., the automobile industry; the steel industry.

industry-

> 2. any general business activity; commercial enterprise.

Throughout my conversations, there was no mention of overarching Industries, as in market spaces in which similar companies compete. The idea of *Industry* is a broad over-generalization. The fact is, *Industries* don't exist. In their place, *industry*—as in any general business activity (and almost always more than one)—stands. When I turned to the Dictionary, I found that this was the same difference between "Industry" in its first definition, and "industry" (with a "small I") in its second definition.

The first definition speaks of big, competitive fields ripe for market analysis and of squeezing big dollars. The second, writ small, speaks of struggle, of doing what you can to make a buck. The difference may seem like it is merely semantic, but its implications are profound.

Centuries ago, the Greek philosopher Diogenes made a similar realization when he distinguished between *Man* and *mankind*. In the city, philosophers stood in front of crowds and spoke of Man. "I tell you *Man* is this…" "I tell you *Man* is that…" Diogenes got rather tired of listening to these lectures day after day.

One day, Diogenes decided to teach the other philosophers a lesson. He took a lighted lamp in his hand, and walked along the busiest street in Athens in broad daylight.

"What are you doing?" people asked him.

"Looking for *Man*."

"But, Diogenes, there are men everywhere!"

"Ah, you have said it yourself. There are men, but there is no such thing as *Man*. You needed a lantern, in addition to the sun, to see what a little child already knows."

Likewise, I think we are all deeply in need of a modern Diogenes to walk down Wall Street with a lamp in hand, to illuminate to people that there is no *Industry*. The "State of the Industry" reports, competitive benchmarking comparisons, and market analyses are flawed. These reports don't show apples-to-apples comparisons, but apples to oranges, pineapples, and bananas. They are fruit salad reports—and about as useful as looking at a bowl of your Grandma's fruit salad in illuminating the predicted future of markets.

The Fortune 500 list now has 70 distinct industries, including "Miscellaneous." Despite such overly-general categories as "metals," 3M, Harley-Davidson, Mattel, Corning, Spectrum Group, and Mohawk Industries are described in terms of belonging to a "Miscellaneous" industry. And what have they got in common? This is a lot like having a filing system where you take every 100th file and throw it into the junk drawer along with your paper clips and rubber bands. I know people who do this—but they aren't usually the people who I would trust find things again later.

Fortune 500 Classification

1	Advertising, Marketing
2	Aerospace and Defense
3	Airlines
4	Apparel
5	Automotive Retailing, Services
6	Beverages
7	Chemicals
8	Commercial Banks
9	Computer Peripherals
10	Computer Software
11	Computers, Office Equipment
12	Construction and Farm Machinery
13	Diversified Financials
14	Diversified Outsourcing Services
15	Education
16	Electronics, Electrical Equipment
17	Energy
18	Engineering, Construction
19	Entertainment
20	Financial Data Services
21	Food and Drug Stores
22	Food Consumer Products
23	Food Production
24	Food Services
25	Forest and Paper Products
26	General Merchandisers
27	Health Care: Insurance and Managed Care
28	Health Care: Medical Facilities
29	Health Care: Pharmacy and Other Services
30	Home Equipment, Furnishings
31	Homebuilders
32	Hotels, Casinos, Resorts
33	Household and Personal Products
34	Industrial Machinery
35	Information Technology Services
36	Insurance: Life, health (mutual)
37	Insurance: Life, health (stock)

38	Insurance: Property and Casualty (mutual)
39	Insurance: Property and Casualty (stock)
40	Internet Services and Retailing
41	Mail, Package, and Freight Delivery
42	Medical Products and Equipment
43	Metals
44	Mining, Crude Oil Production
45	Miscellaneous
46	Motor Vehicles and Parts
47	Network and Other Communications Equipment
48	Oil and Gas Equipment, Services
49	Packaging, Containers
50	Petroleum Refining
51	Pharmaceuticals
52	Pipelines
53	Publishing, Printing
54	Railroads
55	Scientific, Photographic and Control Equipment
56	Securities
57	Semiconductors and Other Electronic Components
58	Specialty Retailers: Apparel
59	Specialty Retailers: Other
60	Telecommunications
61	Temporary Help
62	Tobacco
63	Transportation and Logistics
64	Trucking, Truck Leasing
65	Utilities: Gas and Electric
66	Waste Management
67	Wholesalers: Diversified
68	Wholesalers: Electronics and Office Equipment
69	Wholesalers: Food and Grocery
70	Wholesalers: Healthcare

A still-further challenge is the usefulness of this classification system. In a set of 70 categories which includes categories such as "Publishing, "Printing," "Software," "Internet Services and Retailing," and "Temporary Help," how would one go about classifying a business like Amazon, which might fall into any of the above—given its publishing services, cloud services, online retail books and merchandise trades, and mechanical turk workforce—to say nothing of the emerging industries it is seeking to enter (grocery delivery, for example, or same day delivery via drone).

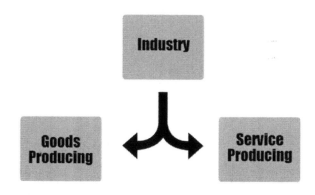

North American Industry Classification System (NAICS)

Other systems are equally damaged. Looking at another classification system—the North American Industry Classification System (NAICS), which is a standard system used by the governments of the U.S., Canada, and Mexico, as well as many private sector businesses—each industry is classified into categories of either Goods-Producing or Service-Providing Industries.

Yet, in reality, the distinction is not so hard-and-fast. What about Software-as-a-service providers who create software, which is provided on a subscription basis as a service? What about all the learning management software companies who make their real money by providing implementation services? What about salons which sell fancy shampoos? What about Bob Evans restaurants which also sell furniture? The list goes on...

OSHA's job codes consist of 99 industry groups in 10 broad categories to create a rainbow of industry classifications.

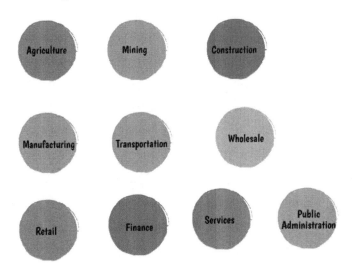

Yet, the industry classifications range from "Miscellaneous Manufacturing Industries," to "Miscellaneous Retail," "Miscellaneous Services," and "Nonclassifiable Establishments." Using the term "nonclassifiable" does not seem much different than "miscellaneous." O*net, a resource sponsored by the U.S. government to help companies define occupational roles for job descriptions, and find out the going pay rate, uses a list of 22 industry codes including "Other services" for a particular role, and "All Industries" to define what skills an employee would need to have in order to successfully fill a job role. Unfortunately, since O*net assumes that there are stable, well-defined industries, and maps job skill sets from those traditional industry definitions, there exist large gaps between the skills that are needed to actually do the jobs within specific competitive niches. For example, computational engineering jobs require knowledge of both engineering concepts and computer science applications, in order to build specialized modelling and simulation software used by engineers. Likewise, the financial engineering jobs rising in popularity on Wall Street require knowledge of engineering methods, mathematical or statistical tools, and software programming to develop financial market models and instruments. Yet, O*net fails to describe careers that exist at the intersection of disciplines and industries. As companies continue to thrive through pursuing competitive niches—which exist in the space between general industries—jobs will continue to become more specialized, more interdisciplinary, and more inter-industry in scope.

It is for this reason that almost every job you joined probably had a steep learning curve—even if you've already held the same job somewhere else before. Each company operates in its unique niche, has its own jargon, and customers to serve. Each company has its own systems, operations, policies, and ways of doing things. And while you may well have the core skill set for the work—having studied it in school and done the job elsewhere—it is in no way the same job as it was at another company. Your past performance on a job elsewhere doesn't well predict your future success, because it isn't the exact same job—even though you might well hold the same title and work in the same broader industry.

Moreover, while O*net job definitions rely on traditionally defined industries, the chances that an individual employee has *all* of these skillsets in a niche is far less likely than the chance of an individual having one or a few of these skills. For example, if 1 out of the 3 software programmers you interview has a skill in programming in Language A (an extremely optimistic and unlikely estimate, I might note), and 1 out of the 3 software programmers you interview has experience using programming Language B, the chances you will find someone who is fluent in Language A *and* Language B is not 1/3 but 1/9 (1/3 x 1/3)! This number is still more likely to drop if you add more skills to the mix (and what job today has just two job-related skills that it is searching for?). If you subsequently actually test the candidates' abilities or require a certain level of proficiency in Language A and Language B, this number is likely to drop still lower, since many candidates might be able to "talk the talk," but are often unable to "walk the walk." It is no wonder, then, that recruiters fail to fill 1/3 of jobs today!

Beyond that, providing a pay scale based on one or another skill set doesn't fairly value the rarity of one who holds all of the required multiple skills *simultaneously*. Although in a general pool of the workforce it may be somewhat rare to find someone with an engineering background, or somewhat rare to find someone with a finance background, it is astronomically rarer to have a financial engineering background. Despite that, few companies actually pay a rate that recognizes this rarity of niche skills, and the cost savings of not having to employ multiple individuals to complete the work required for the single job role.

So if the traditional tools don't work in today's conditions, what's a company to do? The trouble is, companies have come to rely on these faulty analyses for almost everything— from benchmarking performance against competitors, to estimates of how much to invest in R&D or training, to how to develop their own leaders! But just as Diogenes discovered there is no "Man," just "men" (and women), on the larger scale, there is no "Industry," just "industry"—the hard work that companies do in order to find some sort of niche and turn a profit. Looking to the broader market to determine how to make money simply won't help. If companies look to competitors at all, they should be looking to see what they *don't currently do*—because that's how a company will really make money. As the saying goes, "There's riches in niches."

Exercise IX: Flipping Our Benchmarking!

Guiding Questions

1. Who are our largest competitors?

2. What are the top 3 activities which each competitor is engaged in?

3. What niches do these activities serve? (i.e., Midwestern Drill Bit Manufacturers with 50 or more employees, consumers with annual spending on outdoor equipment over $5000)

4. Looking over the list, are there niches that have been missed? For example, could the companies take their current offering and meet the needs of another set of customers? (i.e., if a company is focused on Midwestern Drill Bit Manufacturers with 50 or more employees, could they conceivably spread their business to Western Drill Bit Manufacturers with 50 or more employees? Or what about Midwestern Drill Bit Manufacturers with 100 or more employees?)

5. Looking over the same list, are there any activities that are related to what these firms do, but which have been missed? (i.e., if a company currently supplies drill bits, what about also supplying screws for the drills? Or packages of replacement parts for the drills, since many parts wear out at the same time as the drill bit?)

Flipping Our Benchmarking! Worksheet

Largest Competitor

Activity 1	Activity 2	Activity 3
•**Example:** Drilling	•**Example:** Digging	•**Example:** Panning for Gold

What are the top activities in which this competitor is engaged?

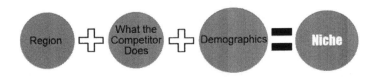

Who are the clients these activities ultimately serve?

[ ]

Are there any geographic boundaries for this customer base?

[ ]

Are there additional regions of this customer base for which we could provide the service?

[ ]

Could these same activities be profitably provided to a different customer base?

Are there any activities that have been missed or overlooked that could be provided profitably to the current customer base?

10 | Homecoming: Environment Shifts Culture

"Turn your wounds into wisdom." –Oprah Winfrey

No human stands apart from the society in which he or she lives. Galileo lived during the time of the Bubonic Plague, which affected everyone in Italy, directly or indirectly. For Galileo, the plague meant delays in publishing, a quarantine of his daughter, and restrictions on travel.

Likewise, no company stands totally separate from the events and context of its market. Rather, these unforeseen and unexpected trials can be formative, and actually serve to shape the culture—sometimes even paving the way for future success. At one consumer goods manufacturing company I visited, when I asked why they did things the way that they did—for example, following certain procedures, and being very careful with their finances despite being quite successful—I was repeatedly presented with a story.

Several decades ago, the company had been a darling of Wall Street, and life was good. The company had commissioned a brand-new skyscraper designed by a famous architect to provide state-of-the-art office space for their growing headquarters. Their CEO began to collect jets like some kids collect baseball cards. Executives were photographed for feature spreads in *Fortune* magazine, quoted as gurus in *The Wall Street Journal,* and greatly admired. Even as the economy began to slow for many companies, demand for their company's products generally remained strong. Then, for the first time in years, the weather didn't cooperate in spurring consumer demand for their seasonal products and people didn't buy.

"No problem," said the then-CEO. "There's never going to be a time when our products are not needed. We'll just keep the inventory and wait until next year."

But the next year, the weather didn't cooperate, either. This situation was unheard-of in the company's long and storied history. But the then-CEO was hopeful that things would turn around. In fact, despite the high inventory, he made an executive decision to keep production running at full-tilt, hoping to squeeze cost out of the product by maintaining the factories' full capacity. While he took a gamble, his reasoning seemed solid. "Look, there has never been a time when the weather has *not* cooperated three years in a row in the whole company's long history. What are the chances? A million to one?"

And then, that million to one hit. The company had almost no sales and no cash flow, as they continued borrowing in order to stay in business. And despite selling their jets and new office tower, they didn't have money to make the bills. Looking at the books, there was no way to make payroll and pay the utilities, taxes, and basic expenses of running their company. So despite having lived off of the bank's credit for the past couple of years, they called their bank and asked their bankers to extend more credit. There was no reason that the bankers should have. In fact, looking at the books, the bank had *every reason* to take the company's assets as collateral and just start dismantling the company to recoup their loss. Indeed, after looking at the books, the bank even initiated discussions to pull financing.

But because the bankers *liked* the company's people, company representatives somehow managed to negotiate for more time. Looking at the situation, there was no objective reason in the world that the company was given more time, and no real evidence that giving the company more time would turn things around. Yet, somehow, they worked a miracle and everybody won.

Those within the company today attribute the bank's extension of credit to the company's *people*. When things were bad, the only thing that stood between corporate survival and devastating bankruptcy including dismantling the company, was its *people*. And the lesson that the company took from this incident was that their people mattered. Ever since, the company has emphasized its "people values."

A Director recounted:

> In my sense in having worked with other companies, it's a very strong culture; very self-severe individuals who have good hometown values. In fact, the company puts a strong emphasis on our corporate values. So there was a point in history where the organization went through a very difficult time, a couple decades ago and almost went under, and the president made a very good decision at that time to define what he thought the corporate values were and really diffuse them throughout the organization. It's become a strong foundation of this organization that is woven into so many different things.

In the words of a Vice President:

> I think that we first care for people and believe that people ultimately drive interaction with customers and customer satisfaction drives good business. From a leadership standpoint, we believe our culture is caring and that drives into relationships with employees, customers, suppliers, our distribution channel, and that has supported us well before I was here.

In one manifestation, that meant that there was no mandatory retirement age within the company. In the words of an Operations Director:

> We just had a guy retire here after 50 years with the company. The longest we've had is 62 years. One of the guys was 88 and still working here. So that gets to be tough, and we kind of blocked him off. "OK, you run this machine, run this job every day," because it really doesn't do us any good to put him on a machine where he's setting up or making changes because he'd probably crash the machine which would cost us thousands of dollars.

Allowing 88 year olds to work in manufacturing is generally unheard-of. When I asked a Training Specialist in another manufacturing company if their company had a culture of retention, I was told:

> No, there is no retention culture. Retention for the sake of it? No. No, there isn't anything like that; improvements are pretty much by the market and bottom line.

The difference between the firms was that the manufacturing company with the strong retention culture had learned from their environment and their difficult market conditions—and had changed their *culture* because of it.

Lessons from the environment matter. These lessons can be terrible jolts from the market, which once survived, serve to make a company stronger. Or these lessons can be behaviors which are richly rewarded by the market, time and time again. No matter the initial cause, these lessons from the environment change the company, transforming its behaviors, its values, and its "ways of doing things."

For example, if your company is heavily focused on serving a single niche, and for whatever reason, demand drops, chances are, you might diversify the market niches that you serve. This diversification of products and offerings—or this lesson from the environment—does not simply "hedge your bet," against market risk, but potentially changes the profile of the customers whom you serve, your approach to serving those customers, and your business focus. Over time, these changes go the very heart of your company. Based on these guiding corporate culture values, key decisions are made. People peg their work to these guiding values.

- "What's the right thing to do?"
- "Who is the most important customer?" (internal or external)
- "Why do we do what we do?"

The answers to these questions form the basis for decisions. They are values questions, and these values are embedded in company culture. There's no "right" answer, except in the context of the company culture. For this company, people come first and foremost. As a result, there's no mandatory retirement age, team contributions are valued more than individual contributions, and camaraderie matters.

For another company, it may be the case that profits come first, in order to meet the needs of shareholders and investors in order to promote continued investment. As a result, a company may place heavy focus on lean sigma and process improvement, have a results orientation, and focus on profitability.

Whatever lessons a company learns from its environment fundamentally change the culture of the company. This transformation doesn't shift a company overnight, but it does change "the way we are." It becomes encoded in the rules, routines, norms, and processes of operating.

Interestingly, this is not a one-time event. Every major shift from the market can drive *organizational learning*. These lessons transform culture, which serve as a way of being. This way of *being*—"the way we are around here"—fundamentally shapes a company's ways of *doing*. A company's approach to key activities—whether how they manage knowledge assets, who the ultimate customer is, what strategies a company pursues for growth, or how they engage their employees—are all influenced by company culture. But these activities also serve as modes for learning. Eventually, these activities serve as a form of *becoming*—where the company is going, and who the company will become in the future. This ultimately changes the company culture, in a (hopefully!) never-ending learning cycle.

One classic management experiment demonstrates the longevity of organizational learning excellently. The experiment involved having participants play a game, in which they would be rewarded for completing a task. During the game, one dominant group participant suggested that the group do things in a particular way—his way. Pretty soon, everyone in the group was approaching the task in the same way, even six "generations" of turnover after the original participant—and all those who had collaborated with the original participant—had left the group. This suggests that change is lasting and that groups are far more stable in their ways of doing things than individuals who are far less bound by group pressures and continuity.

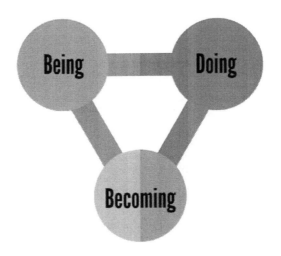

Company ways of doing things are more stable than individual approaches, because people will do work in unfamiliar ways if that's what is needed for the greater good. If an individual needs to deliver a work output to another group, he or she is shaped by what the receiving group needs —what format it needs to be in, when it needs to be delivered, and how to deliver it. Because of these interdependencies, teams' and organizations' actions are much more predictable than an individual's actions—which largely depend upon whim or mood. Instead, there is a logic that exists in the company's "ways of doing," which shapes the behaviors that are deemed appropriate. But despite continuity, major changes or lessons from the environment can transform an organization—often for the better.

It is important to recognize these lessons from the environment for what they are, and to honor the culture that it has created, rather than to introduce change simply for change's sake. It is my hope that you will more deeply examine the real world data of your company—and that you, too, will experience a Galileo Moment.

Exercise X: Understanding Our Company

Company Culture

- What is the core of our being?
- Compared to competitors, what makes our company unique?
- Are there any company stories which illustrate our core values?
- If there was a sudden downturn, what budgeted item would be the last to go?

Client Focus

- *Who* is all this for?
- Who is the client who is ultimately being served?
- If trade-offs had to be made, which stakeholder would get what they want?

Growth Strategy

- Do we prefer steady growth or an accelerated pace?
- What is the most important outcome of growth?
- To what extent does protecting our company culture matter?

Knowledge Management

- How do we remember information?
- How do we connect people to the information resources that they need when they need it?
- Where do we strike the balance between *exploitation* of previously known information, and *exploration* of learning new things?

<u>Engagement</u>

- What do we do to engage our employees?
- How do we recognize employee efforts?
- Why do employees decide to work for us, rather than for our competition?

<u>Organizational Learning</u>

- What market events have been formative in our company's history?
- Knowing what we know now, what should we do differently?
- In what way might we transform a negative event into a positive?

APPENDIX: Exercise Workbook

Exercise I: Preparing for Your Galileo Moment

STEP 1		**CHECK YOUR LENSES** Am I looking at real-world data & evidence, or am I filtering the data?
STEP 2		**LOOK INSIDE** What additional data do I need in order to make an informed decision?
STEP 3		**LOOK OUTSIDE** Who else does this impact?
STEP 4		**LOOK BEYOND** What is the risk of continuing to do what I have been doing?

What lenses am I looking through? Am I looking at real-world data, or am I filtering information?

| |
| |
| |

What additional data do I need to make an informed decision?

| |
| |
| |

Who else does this impact?

| |
| |
| |

What is the risk of continuing to do what I have been doing?

| |
| |
| |

If I intend to make a change, how do I know it is the right change? Am I following a scientific method in a data-driven manner when making changes, or am I making multiple changes such that I cannot measure the impact of those changes and make adjustments?

| |
| |
| |

Exercise II: Succinctly Defining Our Company Culture

Use the **Guiding Questions** to come up with a **Succinct Definition** of your company culture.

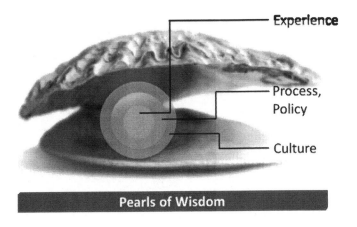

Guiding Questions

Where have we been and what did we learn?

1) What were the key, defining moments in our company's history?

| |
| |
| |
| |

2) What did we learn from these moments?

| |
| |
| |
| |

3) What other lessons might we have taken from these
    moments in our company's history?

<table>
<tr><td></td></tr>
<tr><td></td></tr>
<tr><td></td></tr>
</table>

How do we <u>DO</u> business?

1) What is our client focus?

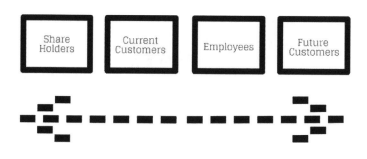

2) What type of growth strategy are we pursuing?

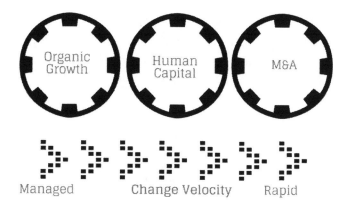

3) How do we manage knowledge?

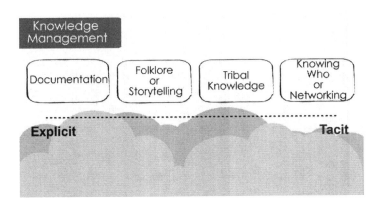

4) How do we engage our employees?

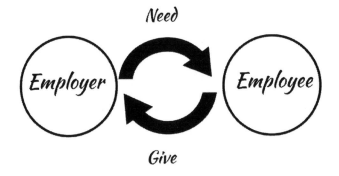

Succinct Definition

Choose 5-10 words to write a succinct definition of your company culture.

Review

Once you have done this, your work still isn't finished. Now consider: would managers in other groups or employees agree with this definition? If not, take this opportunity to revise. What we are looking for is not a description of the way we *wish it would be*, but *how people feel it really is*, in order to serve as an accurate starting point or "ground zero" for discussions and strategizing. Once you have succinctly defined your culture, it will become much easier to determine strategy, tactics, and implementation.

Exercise III: Digging into Resistance to Change

When processes change, it sometimes requires a change in mental models or mindset as well as changing the process itself. Communicating this change and why the change is required now may help ease the transition, since ways of doing things are intimately connected with company culture.

Since change is a constant in any living company, it is often necessary to pinpoint the actual root cause of resistance, in order to better address why the change is encountering resistance. To do so, ask the following questions:

- **Are you encountering resistance to change?**
- **If so, is the resistance coming from a handful of vocal people, or is it distributed more broadly?**
- **Can you pin point the cause of organizational resistance? (See 6 causes of organizational resistance)**

6 Causes of Organizational Resistance

Defensive routines

- Is the issue personally embarrassing?

- Why don't you think things will change?

Success Bias

- Have we been successful in this area in the past?

- What would happen if we approached things completely differently?

Departmental Siloing

- Why do we feel that the situation is "us" versus "them"?

- Are the departments being rewarded for different outcomes?

- How do department leaders' personalities shape each of the groups?

Cognitive Rigidities

- Why are things done this way?

- What were the reasons behind it?

- Are these reasons still relevant now?

- What has changed since we put the process or policy in place?

Groupthink and reduced process conflict

- Is "getting along with others" rewarded?

- Are there ways in which we could better reward innovative behaviors?

Contradicting Company Culture

- Do the new processes or changes conflict with company culture?

- Is there a way to take a gradual approach to slowly change in order to adapt to the proposed change?

- Is the change really necessary? How necessary is it to make this particular change now? What would happen if this change were not made?

Exercise IV: Defining Our Ultimate Stakeholder

Who is your Ultimate Stakeholder? (If a hard decision had to be made, and not everyone could get what they wanted, who would ultimately get what they want?)

Who is your Ultimate Stakeholder? (If a hard decision had to be made, and not everyone could get what they wanted, who would ultimately get what they want?)

What is the time orientation of serving this stakeholder? (Is it a quarterly orientation or span of decades?)

What are the risks involved in serving this stakeholder?

How can these risks be minimized?

What are the limitations of focusing on this stakeholder?

Exercise V: Defining Our Product/Service Offering

For *each* product or service offering, chart where your company's offering lies along the continuum.

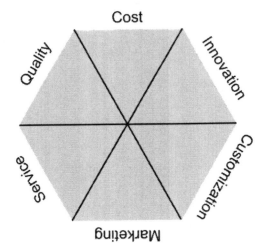

Instructions:

To complete this grid, think of each segment as its own continuum. Locate **high** values towards the outer edges of the hexagon. Locate **low values** (or **narrow values**) closest toward the center of the hexagon.

1. Where does your offering currently fall along the cost continuum?

   Low   High

   ←——————————————————————→

2. Where does your offering currently fall along the innovation continuum?

   Low   High

   ←——————————————————————→

3. Where does your offering currently fall along the marketing continuum?

   Low   High

   ←——————————————————————→

4. Where does your offering currently fall along the customization continuum?

   Low   High

   ←——————————————————————→

5. Where does your offering currently fall along the service continuum?

Low   High

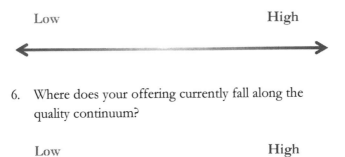

6. Where does your offering currently fall along the quality continuum?

Low   High

Exercise VI: Analyzing Risk Trade-Off

Decision
Trade-Offs

Speed	Accuracy
Cutting Edge Product	Broad Market Acceptance of Product
Innovation	Reliability
Quality	Cost
Niche Customer Loyalty	Market Share
Diversity	Hierarchy
Lean Operations	Redundancy of Systems Leading to Stability
Per Unit Costs with Reduced Risk in Downturn	Fixed Costs with Potential Profitability
Purchase Acquisitions	Innovate Internally
Employee Loyalty and Increased Organizational Citizenship	Flexible Labor as Employees
Nimble Decisions	Large Company Size
Team Work	Autonomy
Internal Control of Business	External Funding
Employee Work/Life Balance	24/7 Customer Support
Process Improvement and Agility	Process Documentation
Future Profits	Current Cash Assets

1) Which risks do you currently manage? **(list out)**

```



```

2) What are the potential risks or trade-offs that result from managing that risk?

```



```

3) Are these acceptable risks? What is the alternative?

```



```

Exercise VII: Coordinating Decisioning

Tools:

1. What $ amount, or $ amount out of budget should people come to you for?

2. What types of risk?

3. What time? (At risk of being over schedule? at a certain amount of time overschedule? for a project that will take up a certain amount or percent of job time?)

4. Impact on others outside of function? (Is it outside of project scope? does it involve changes outside of particular product?)

Decisioning

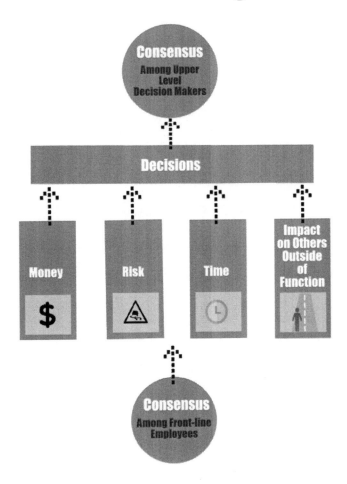

Exercise VIII: Rating Our Octane

Low Octane ← → High Octane

1. How refined (or what octane) does your idea fuel need to be?

2. What are the company's current capabilities?

3. How will the ideas be communicated across the organization?

4. How long will an idea remain in the repository before being reviewed, revised, or rejected?

Exercise IX: Flipping Our Benchmarking!

Guiding Questions

1. Who are our largest competitors?

2. What are the top 3 activities which each competitor is engaged in?

3. What niches do these activities serve?

   (i.e., Midwestern Drill Bit Manufacturers with 50 or more employees, consumers with annual spending on outdoor equipment over $5000)

4. Looking over the list, are there niches that have been missed? For example, could the companies take their current offering and meet the needs of another set of customers? (i.e., if a company is focused on Midwestern Drill Bit Manufacturers with 50 or more employees, could they conceivably spread their business to Western Drill Bit Manufacturers with 50 or more employees? Or what about Midwestern Drill Bit Manufacturers with 100 or more employees?)

5. Looking over the same list, are there any activities that are related to what these firms do, but which have been missed? (i.e., if a company currently supplies drill bits, what about also supplying screws for the drills? Or packages of replacement parts for the drills, since many parts wear out at the same time as the drill bit?)

Flipping Our Benchmarking! Worksheet

Largest Competitor

Activity 1

- **Example:** Drilling

Activity 2

- **Example:** Digging

Activity 3

- **Example:** Panning for Gold

What are the top activities in which this competitor is engaged?

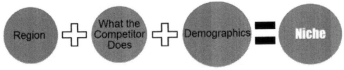

Who are the clients these activities ultimately serve?

Are there any geographic boundaries for this customer base?

Are there additional regions of this customer base for which we could provide the service?

Could these same activities be profitably provided to a different customer base?

```

```

Are there any activities that have been missed or overlooked that could be provided profitably to the current customer base?

```

```

Exercise X: Understanding Our Company

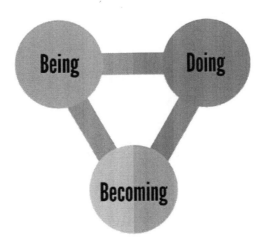

Company Culture

- What is the core of our being?
- Compared to competitors, what makes our company unique?
- Are there any company stories which illustrate our core values?
- If there was a sudden down turn, what budgeted item would be the last to go?

Client Focus

- *Who* is all this for?
- Who is the client who is ultimately being served?
- If trade-offs had to be made, which stakeholder would get what they want?

Growth Strategy

- Do we prefer steady growth or an accelerated pace?
- What is the most important outcome of growth?
- To what extent does protecting our company culture matter?

Knowledge Management

- How do we remember information?
- How do we connect people to the information resources that they need when they need it?
- Where do we strike the balance between *exploitation* of previously known information, and exploration of learning new things?

Engagement

- What do we do to engage our employees?
- How do we recognize employee efforts?
- Why do employees decide to work for us, rather than our competition?

Organizational Learning

- What market events have been formative in our company's history?
- Knowing what we know now, what should we do differently?
- In what way might we transform a negative event into a positive?

Sources

Ashkenas, R. (2013). Change management needs to change. *Harvard Business Review.*

Argyris, C. 1999. *On Organizational Learning,* (2nd ed.) Malden, MA: Blackwell Business.

Bjerke, B. & Hultman, C.M. (2002). *Entrepreneurial marketing: The growth of small firms in the new economic era.* Cheltenham, UK: Edward Elgar Publishing Limited.

Chang, Y.Y. & Hughes, M. (2012). Drivers of innovation ambidexterity in small to medium sized firms. *European Management Journal, 30,* 1-17.

Daft, R.L. & Weick, K.E. (1984). Toward a model of organizations as interpretation systems. *Academy of Management Review, 9*(2), 284-295.

de Geus, A.P. (1988). Planning as learning. *Harvard Business Review, 66,* 70-74.

Dess, G.G. & Beard, D.W. (1984). Dimensions of organizational task environments. *Administrative Science Quarterly, 29*(1), 52-73.

Ebner, W., Leimeister, J.M., Krcmar, H. (2009). Community engineering for innovations: the ideas competition as a method to nurture a virtual community for innovations. *R&D Management, 39*(4), 342-356. DOI: 10.1111/j.1467-9310.2009.00564.x

Ford, R. (2008). Organizational learning, change, and power: Toward a practice-theory framework. *Journal of Change Management, 8*(3-4), 173-198.

Ford, D.N., Voyer, J.J., & Wilkinson, J.M.G. (2000). Building learning organizations in engineering cultures: Case study. *Journal of Management in Engineering, 16*(4), 72-83.

Forrester, J.W. (1961). *Industrial Dynamics.* Waltham, MA: Pegasus Communications.

Garrido, P. (2009). Business sustainability and collective intelligence. *The Learning Organization, 16*(3), 208-222. DOI 10.1108/09696470910949935

Gassman, O., Enkel, E., & Chesbrough, H. (2010). The future of open innovation. *R&D Management, 40*(3), 213-221. DOI: 10.1111/j.1467-9310.2010.00605.x

Grey, B., Sheelagh, M., Boshoff, C., & Matheson, P. (1998). Developing a better measure of market orientation. *European Journal of Marketing, 32*(9/10), 884-903.

Heraty, N. & Morley, M. (2008). Dimensionalizing the architecture of organization-led learning: A framework for collective practice. *Advances in Developing Human Resources, 10*(4), 472-493.DOI: 10.1177/1523422308320471

Herriot, S.R., Levinthal, D., & March, J.G. (1985). Learning from experience in organizations. *American Economic Review, 75*(2), 298-302.

Huber, G.P. (1991). Organizational learning: The contributing processes and the literatures. *Organization Science, 2,* 88-115.

Hutchins, E. (1991). Organizing work by adaptation. *Organization Science, 2*(1), 14-39.

Jayanti, E.B. (2011a). Through a different lens: A survey of linear epistemological assumptions underlying HRD models. *Human Resource Development Review,* 10(1), 101-114. DOI: 10.1177/1534484310386753.

Jayanti, E.B. (2011b). Towards pragmatic criteria for evaluating HRD research. *Human Resource Development Review,* *10*(4), 431-450. DOI: 10.1177/1534484311412723

Jayanti, E. (2012). Open sourced organizational learning: Implications and challenges of crowdsourcing for human resource development (HRD) practitioners. *Human Resource Development International,* 1-10. DOI: 10.1080/13678868.2012.669235

Kahneman, D., Slovic, P. & Tversky, A. (1982). *Judgment under uncertainty: Heuristics and biases.* New York, NY: Cambridge University Press.

Kale, P., Singh, H. & Perlmutter, H. (2000). Learning and protection of property assets in strategic alliances: Building relational capital. *Strategic Management Journal,* *21*(3), 217-237.

Kenny, J. (2006). Strategy and the learning organization: A maturity model for the formation of strategy. *The Learning Organization,* *13*(4), 353-368. DOI 10.1108/09696470610667733

Levitt, B. & March, J.G. (1988). Organizational learning. *Annual Review of Sociology*, 14, 319-340.

Love, P.E.D., Li, H., Irani, Z. & Faniran, O. (2000). Total quality management and the learning organization: A dialogue for change in construction. *Construction Management and Economics*, *18*(3), 321-331. DOI: 10.1080/014461900370681

March, J.G. (1991). Exploration and exploitation in organizational learning. *Organization Science*, *2*(1), 71-87.

March, J.G. & Simon, H.A. (1993). *Organizations*. Oxford, UK: Blackwell.

Marsick, V.J., & Watkins, K.E. (2003). Demonstrating the value of an organization's learning culture: The Dimensions of the Learning Organization Questionnaire. *Advances in Developing Human Resources*, *5*(2), 132-151. DOI: 10.1177/1523422303251341

Massingham, P. & Diment, K. (2009). Organizational commitment, knowledge management interventions, and learning organization capacity. *The Learning Organization*, *16* (2), 122-142. DOI: 10.1108/09696470910939206

Mckinley, W. & Scherer, A.G. (2000). Some unanticipated consequences of organizational restructuring. *Academy of Management Review, 4*, 735-752.

Moorman, C. & Miner, A.S. (1998). Organizational improvisation and organizational memory. *Academy of Management Review, 23*, 698-723.

Narver, J.C. & Slater, S.F. (1990). The effect of a market orientation on business profitability. *Journal of Marketing, 54*, 20-35.

Nonaka, I. (1991). The knowledge-creating company. *Harvard Business Review,* November-December, 96-104.

Nystrom, P.C. & Starbuck, W.H. (1984). To avoid organizational crises, unlearn. *Organizational Dynamics, 12*, 53-65.

Ortenblad, A. (2005). Are the right persons involved in the creation of the learning organization? *Human Resource Development Quarterly, 16*(2), 281-283.

Paap, J. & Katz, R. (2004). Anticipating disruptive innovation. *Research Technology Management, 47*(5), 13-22.

Sackmann, S. (1992). Culture and subcultures: An analysis of organizational knowledge. *Administrative Science Quarterly, 37*(1), 140-161.

Schein, E.H. (1999). Empowerment, coercive persuasion, and organizational learning: Do they connect? *The Learning Organization, 6*(4), 163-172.

Schreyogg, G. & Sydow, J. (2010). Organizing for fluidity? Dilemmas of new organizational forms. *Organization Science, 21*(6), 1251-1262. DOI: 10.1287/orsc.1100.0561

Senge, P.M. (1990). *The fifth discipline.* New York, NY: Doubleday.

Simon, H. A. (1955). A behavioral model of rational choice. *Quarterly Journal of Economics, 69*, 99–118.

Simon, H.A. (1991). Bounded rationality and organizational learning. *Organization Science, 2*(1), 125-134.

Simonin, B.L. (1997). The importance of collaborative know-how: An empirical test of the learning organization. *Academy of Management Journal, 40*(5), 1150-1174.

Sinkula, J.M. (1994). Market information processing and organizational learning. *Journal of Marketing, 58*, 35-45.

Slater, S.F. & Narver, J.C. (1995). Market orientation and the learning organization. *Journal of Marketing, 59*, 63-74.

Snell, R.S. (2001). Moral foundations of the learning organization. *Human Relations, 54*(3), 319-342. DOI: 10.1177/0018726701543003

Spender, J.C. (1996). Making knowledge the basis of a dynamic theory of the firm. *Strategic Management Journal, 17*, 45-62.

Stacey, R. (2003). Learning as an activity of interdependent people. *Learning Organization, 10*(6), 325-331. DOI 10.1108/09696470310497159

Steers, R.M. (1975). Problems in the measurement of organizational effectiveness. *Administrative Science Quarterly, 20*(4), 546-558.

Sternberg, R.J. & Grigorenko, E.L. (1997). Are cognitive styles still in style? *American Psychologist, 52*(7), 700-712.

Taleb, N.N. (2012). *Antifragile: Things that Gain from Disorder.* New York, NY: Random House.

Tellis, G.J., Prabhu, J.C. & Chandy, R.K. (2009). Radical innovation across nations: The preeminence of Corporate Culture. *Journal of Marketing, 73*(1), 3-23.

Thagard, P. (2005). *Mind: Introduction to Cognitive Science*, (2nd Ed.). Cambridge, MA: MIT Press.

Tsuchiya, S. (2011). In search of effective methodology for organizational learning: A Japanese experience. *Simulation and Gaming, 42*(3), 384-396. DOI: 10.1177/1046878111401843

Tversky, A. & Kahneman, D. (1986). Rational choice and framing of decisions. *Journal of Business, 59*, S251-S278.

Van de Ven, A.H. & Poole, M.S. (2005). Alternative approaches for studying organizational change. *Organization Studies, 26*, 1377-1396.

Wang, T. (2004). From General System theory to Total Quality Management. *Journal of American Academy of Business, 4*(1/2), 394-400.

Waterman, R.H. (1987). *The renewal factor: How the best get and keep the competitive edge.* Toronto, Canada: Bantam Books.

Weick, K.E. (1969). *The social psychology of organizing.* Reading, MA: Addison-Wesley.

Weick, K. & Roberts, K. (1993). Collective mind in organizations: Heedful interrelating on flight decks. *Administrative Science Quarterly, 38*(3), 357-381.

Yang, J. (2007). The impact of knowledge sharing on organizational learning and effectiveness. *Journal of Knowledge Management, 11*(2), 84-90. DOI: 10.1108/13673270710738933

Zaki, J. & Oschner, K. (2011). Reintegrating the study of accuracy into social cognition research. *Psychological*